A Message of Hope

FOR SURVIVING THE TRAGEDY OF SUICIDE

by

Patricia Harness-Overley

BRADLEY PRESS

A Message of Hope for Surviving the Tragedy of Suicide

ISBN 0-9634571-0-1

Published by Bradley Press, Upland, California 91786.

For the most part only first names were used in this book. Many of these are fictitious in order to protect the privacy of those people.

Design & Composition by:
Highpoint Graphics, Claremont, California 91711

Printed in the United States of America by:
KNI, Incorporated, Anaheim, California 92806

Acknowledgements

I would like to express my sincere appreciation for the encouragement and support I received from so many people as I worked on this book. It is impossible to name them all individually.

All of the people from the Hope After Suicide support group. You have all helped me in my healing, learning and moving forward with my life.

Karen Brockbank, the sharing of your pain was a tremendous contribution. I will always appreciate the support you and Nancy Roberts have given me.

My friend Mary Jo Sohovich is a wonderful writer. I spent a considerable amount of time asking for her help. She was always there for me with words of encouragement as she made the much needed corrections.

Robert Lefler L.C.S.W. is one of the most kind and sensitive people that I have ever had the privilege of knowing. He read my manuscript numerous times and his input was always helpful. His wife is a school teacher and she also helped. I am grateful to them both.

I thank my family. Especially my son Steve and his wife Jan.

My husband Gene deserves an award for his gentleness and understanding as I relived the hellish nightmare of Brad's death and the years that followed. He encouraged me to keep going when I thought that I couldn't. Without his help there wouldn't be a finished book.

Contents

Chapter One

The Shock

Suicide was something that happened to other families, not to mine. Or so it was until 1984 when my 18-year-old son, Brad, died by his own hand.

Brad lived a few hundred miles away with his father, Larry, at the time of his death. Larry and I had divorced two years earlier.

Alone in the house, I was startled by the ring of the telephone. At first I considered letting the answering machine take the message because I was busy with paperwork and resented the interruption.

When I answered the phone that Sunday afternoon I was surprised to hear my ex-husband's voice. We rarely spoke because of the hostility we felt toward each other. I knew something had to be wrong.

"Pat," he said, "Is Stan there yet?"

"No, he isn't here. Why?"

"Well, I called and asked him to be with you. Are you alone?"

"Yes, I am. What's wrong with you? You're not making any sense."

"Oh well. There isn't an easy way to say this. Pat, Brad is dead."

I couldn't believe what I was hearing. At the same time, I was visualizing an automobile accident.

"Oh, God. No. He's been in an accident," were the words coming from me, but it sounded as if someone else were speaking them.

I was told it was no accident. Brad had shot himself. The greatest pain I've ever known swept over me. All I could think was that it must be a mistake. My baby couldn't be dead!

But it was no mistake. Brad was dead and my life would never be the same.

As I placed the receiver back in its cradle, I became aware of an overwhelming quiet in the house. The only sounds I could hear were the birds singing outside. Why are they singing? Don't they know Brad is dead?

I stood frozen in shock, not knowing what to do. Then I ran from my bedroom, down the stairs to Brad's room, as if looking for him. Standing in the doorway with my arms wrapped around myself, I rocked back and forth, crying and screaming "Oh, God. No! Please don't let it be true! Please, God, please don't let it be true!"

I walked from room to room in the empty house like a caged animal, my arms still wrapped around myself in a futile attempt at protection from the pain. Waves of nausea swept over me. Then, numbness. Knots clogged my throat and twisted my stomach. Nothing seemed real. Surely I was dreaming. Suddenly, I became very cold and started to shake.

As though in a daze, I went to the telephone and called my business partner to explain what had happened and that I would be away from the office for a few days. I then called my sister. She wasn't home.

My mother! How could I possibly tell her that her grandson is dead? She had spent the past five years taking care of my father as he slowly, painfully, died from emphysema.

We weren't a family that could ask for help, at any time. Though financially my mother could have placed Daddy in a rest home, she chose to care for him personally—bathing his frail, 64-pound body, seeing to his every need as best she could.

I placed the call to her, searching for the right words. On the second ring I heard my brother-in-law's voice. I wondered why he was answering my mother's phone.

"Stan, Brad is...." He interrupted me, "Pat, we know about Brad. I've been trying to reach you. When I called your office they said you had gone home for the day. There was no answer at your house either.

Larry called me first so that someone would be with you when he told you. I'll be at your place as fast as I can."

Why hadn't I remembered that Larry had spoken first with Stan? Resentment began to build that so many people knew of Brad's death before I did. Then there was an overpowering need to tell other people what had happened.

The next call was to my best friend and then to other friends.

As I told each person the news, they said, without the least bit of hesitance, "I'll be right there." Soon the house was filled with caring people. I wanted them there and needed their support.

I also wanted them to go away. Their presence meant that Brad's death was a truth.

No more than an hour had passed, but it seemed like a lifetime. I was cold and shaking, and emotionally and physically exhausted.

I went to Brad's room to lie down on his bed. As I looked about, I thought how unlike him this room seemed.

When Brad left to live with his father he took almost everything he owned. Only a few of his clothes remained in the closet. There was little else to give the room his personal touch. There was no unmade bed with clothes thrown over and under it, which ordinarily, Brad would leave in his wake.

The only things that were truly him were his bed and the large American flag he had nailed to the wall over it. With my body curled into a fetal position, knees and chin almost touching, I lay on the bed.

I looked up at the flag through tears. My thoughts screamed, what a lie! Life, liberty, and justice, all lies! Where was Brad's life? Where was his liberty? Where the hell was the justice?

I jumped to my feet and clawed at the flag, trying to rip it from the wall. At the same time, I was screaming every foul word I'd ever heard.

My mother came into the room with a look of helpless terror. Her voice revealed her concern as she said, "Come on Pat. This won't help. You're going to hurt yourself." She reached for me, but I angrily pushed her away.

People were standing in the doorway, not sure how to handle the situation.

My friend Linda, who had just arrived, pushed her way into the room. She jumped onto the bed and grabbed my arms. We fell. She landed on top of me and restrained me so I could not move.

I screamed at her to leave me alone. Her strength amazed me. She held me in a firm, loving manner until I ceased to scream and fight.

Although I did not understand it at the time, I was in shock and denial. Only after the shock subsides does the real grieving begin.

The First Days

The first few days were filled with activity, and I was surrounded by friends and relatives at all times. The telephone seemed to ring constantly. Flowers and cards began to arrive.

I had contacted my older son, Steve, with the help of his wife, Jan. He was a lieutenant in the army, on duty in Turkey. How I hated to inform him of his brother's death.

Only three months earlier he had been called home when my father died. Because Steve and I had lived with my parents for the first nine years of his life, he and his grandfather had been extremely close. They were more like father and son. I knew he was still grieving that loss.

Steve was nearly 11 years older than Brad. Being the eldest, Steve was protective of Brad and loved him in a very special way. The

24-hour flight from Turkey to California must have been dreadful for him emotionally.

The activity going on around me seemed unreal. I had nothing yet to confirm Brad's death.

Larry had informed me that Brad's face was destroyed by the gunshot. We agreed that his body would be cremated.

The wait for my two sons to arrive seemed endless and unbearable. One would come home standing tall and handsome in his uniform, with a wrinkled brow from worry and pain in his heart. The other would arrive in ashes that had been placed in a small box.

What little sleep I got in those first few days and nights was filled with dreams of Brad. One dream recurred every time I dozed off. Brad was lost and I couldn't find him. I felt the panic a mother feels when she thinks her child is lost.

Most people were kind and helpful. These brave, well-meaning friends arrived with a look of concern on their faces. Although they weren't sure of what they should say or do, they had come to offer their help.

I was repeatedly asked how the death had come about and why. I could tell them in part how, but not why, because I didn't know why.

"Brad, of all people," they would say. "He just didn't seem the type."

Brad had a playful nature. He was always laughing and joking and was very sensitive to the needs of others.

This was February and the last time I had seen Brad was the first of January. At that time he didn't laugh or joke around the way he had in the past. Though he seemed more mature, he was also very angry. I tried to find out what was wrong, but he refused to talk about whatever was bothering him. The hurt I saw in his eyes will haunt me for the rest of my life.

My mother accompanied me to the mortuary to plan my son's funeral—the same mortuary where my father had been three months earlier.

We requested the same man who had helped us with the arrangements for my father. He was not working that day, and we were helped instead by the wife of the owner.

She was a lady in her seventies who had obviously been at the job far too long, for she had lost the compassion so necessary to do the job well.

When asked what music we would like, I explained I wasn't sure, but I didn't want it to be sad. Upon hearing this, she became angry and informed me a mortuary wasn't the place for a party.

Even in my numb state I could feel the sting of her insensitive remark. In a weak, monotone voice, I replied, "I'll get back to you about the music."

Later that afternoon I received a call from a friend who expressed how sorry she was to hear of Brad's death and offered her help. This woman has been blessed with the most beautiful singing voice I've ever heard.

I explained to her what had happened earlier at the mortuary. She told me to let her take care of the music.

Carol Hawkins brought me such comfort the day of the funeral. The music she chose was just what I had in mind. Her voice had the pure tone of an angel as she sang "Bridge Over Troubled Water." It was clear to everyone she was singing from her heart.

Those days of awaiting the arrival of my former husband seemed an eternity. When at last I opened the door, he stood there with a very small box in his hand.

As he handed me the box, he said, "You sent me a healthy boy and I bring you back a box of ashes."

I couldn't believe how small that box was. It weighed about five or six pounds. Smaller than Brad had been at birth.

I held the small plastic box to my breast and cried. I felt like the tears would never stop. All day long I held the box close to me, even when we went to the mausoleum.

We were fortunate to find a niche in the same row where my father's crypt is located. It brought me comfort to know they would be near each other. The niche I chose was the center of a cross. This seemed the most appropriate placement, for he had so often been "nailed to the cross" in his young life.

This night, before the funeral, would be my last opportunity to hold my son. I placed the box of ashes in bed with me and cried myself to sleep. I slept without any bad dreams.

Funeral

The day of the funeral I was a zombie. I didn't want this to be happening, but I knew it must be done. It was hard to believe any of it could be true.

The chapel could not accommodate the number of people who attended. It was crowded beyond capacity, and many people remained outside.

I thought, "Oh, Brad, so many people cared about you. Why? Why didn't you tell some of us what was wrong? Why didn't I do more to help you?"

Approximately 60 people came back to my home that day. There was so much food, and I'm not even sure where it all came from.

We talked, we cried, we laughed, and then we cried some more. A few friends stayed all night.

Most everyone was kind and thoughtful. However, it seems there is always one rotten apple in the barrel and we had ours. She was the mother of one of Brad's friends.

Five or six years earlier, her husband had been killed. While she was mourning her husband, her son spent many days and nights in our home. We had a very strong bond with this boy.

The evening of Brad's funeral, she called me and said in a very angry and demanding voice, "You and Larry created this relationship with my son. Larry has let him down by not staying in touch with him. Just because Brad is dead, don't forget about my son!"

Her lack of compassion was apparent, not only with words but in the tone of voice she used. I couldn't believe what I had heard. Retaliation and self-defense were actions I had been very good at in the past, but instead of rebuking her, I found myself reassuring her in the same weak, monotone voice that was becoming a part of me.

Although I was exhausted, sleep would not come to me that night. Thoughts of Brad filled my head. Tears filled my eyes and pain filled my heart. What would life be like without my baby? Would this pain ever stop? Why didn't he want to live? What was he thinking as he pulled the trigger? Why didn't he talk to me?

How could I go on living? I felt I had not protected Brad and had let him down by not being there when he needed me the most.

Brad's young life had not been an easy one. Brad was dyslexic, and although he had a very high IQ, he had been in special education classes in school.

When he was nine years old, he was struck by an automobile. As the result of the accident, he had a brain stem injury, total deafness in his left ear, and paralysis of the left side of his face. When he came home from the hospital, he was also paralyzed on the right side of his body, but with many months of therapy he overcame that handicap.

About one year after the divorce, he became involved with some people a few years older than he was. He stopped attending school on a regular basis and was headed for trouble.

I took him to see a psychologist, who I'd been told specialized in young people with problems. At the first appointment, I told him that Brad would not only lie to him but he would also charm him into believing everything was all right. I was assured that he could handle the problem.

On our third visit, the psychologist informed me that Brad was fine, but I needed to learn to relax or I would develop a health problem.

He was right about my needing to find a way to relax. I had an extreme amount of stress from worry about my son and my own work. But he was wrong about Brad.

I asked Brad's father to help pay for better therapy for Brad and received a reply by mail which stated he would not help because Brad needed discipline, not therapy.

Brad tried to join the army but was turned down because of his loss of hearing. He went to all the other branches of the armed services. None would accept him.

After a weekend visit with his father, Brad told me it had been decided he would live with his father because he wanted to get away from the people he was involved with and finish school.

I had an uneasy feeling about Brad living with his father and step-mother. Larry was an alcoholic. He was extremely critical, insensitive, and at times he could be downright cruel. His wife was the woman he had been involved with at the time of our separation, and she and Brad had an intense dislike for each other.

We discussed these problems. Brad reminded me that Larry had completed a hospital rehabilitation program for his alcoholism and that his grandparents lived nearby so he could spend time with them if he felt a need to be away from his step-mother. He also talked to me about how much he enjoyed his grandfather's ranch.

I agreed that the rural farming community would be a better environment and allowed him to go. He moved, and he did finish school.

Some two months before his death, Brad told me he was unhappy living with his father. He said it was like being in jail, and he asked if he could live with me once more. He had lost a lot of weight. This was good, because he had been too heavy, but he had a troubled look in his eyes. There was a sadness about him.

The emptiness in his eyes told me that I must do something and do it fast. We agreed that he could return home with the condition he attend a trade school.

He told me that he would like to become a cross-country truck driver. Although this was not what I had in mind for him, I said fine and confirmed our plan with his father. We all agreed I was to locate a school, then send for Brad.

When I called them to say everything was set, first Brad, then his father informed me that Brad was not coming home. I repeatedly asked him if he was sure, and he replied, "Yes, I'm sure." The tone in his voice belied those words. After considerable arguing, and with a feeling of frustration, I hung up.

These events went through my mind again and again the night of the funeral.

Life Goes On

The day after the funeral was a much quieter one than the days preceding it had been. There were still calls and cards in the mail. Not as many people stopped by. The excitement was dying down. Their lives were getting back to normal.

One morning I received a call from a client (with a partner, I owned a real estate brokerage). He said he was sorry to hear my son had died. He then expressed concern about his real estate transaction. My partner or any one of our agents could have handled his concerns, but he insisted that I take care of it personally.

Thinking work might be beneficial to me, I went to the office. I went about my tasks like a wind-up toy, still insulated from reality by shock.

Three weeks after the funeral, it was necessary for me to move. The large beautiful house I'd been living in was owned by a bank that had foreclosed on its original owners. My partner and I had sold the house before Brad's death. The escrow was now ready to close.

Decisions that had been easy to make in the past were now extremely difficult. I felt so unsure of myself. Finally I made the decision to look for an apartment. None of them seemed safe. I'd never been this frightened in my entire life. Time was running out and a place had to be found or I would be without a home.

Spotting a nice-looking apartment complex one day, I stopped and went in to talk to the manager.

She was a large, raw-boned woman, about 5 foot 9 and must have weighed 185 pounds or more. I later learned she was an ex-Marine who had served our country with pride in the Korean War.

She gave me the keys to an available apartment, told me it was easy to find, and sent me on my way. The street I was to follow was a simple horseshoe with the apartment opening onto it.

In my confused state of mind, I couldn't find it. So I went back into the office with tears streaming down my face and told her, "My son died two weeks ago. I'm confused and I can't find that damned apartment."

Hearing my words, this large lady took me into her arms. I cried like a baby. I knew I had found a home. The woman and her husband were both very kind to me for the year I lived there.

Moving from the large house was a big undertaking. Thank goodness for the help of family and good friends. I had too much furniture for the apartment. I sold some of it, at far too low a price, and gave a lot away.

"Things" didn't mean much to me without Brad. All the plants I'd enjoyed over the years were given away or thrown out. I told myself and anyone who would listen that I didn't have time to care for them. The truth was, I didn't want anything "living" around me.

Even though Steve had done an excellent job with the painful task of packing and giving away Brad's belongings, I kept finding little things as I packed. A comb with bits of Brad's hair in it caused me to sob uncontrollably for hours.

Steve returned to Turkey. I felt very sad and alone.

The dreams of Brad were unrelenting. Night after night I would awake and feel Brad in the room with me. I would fall back asleep only to have the dreams return.

A dear friend's daughter, with whom Brad had attended school, was to be married. They wanted me to be a guest at the wedding and said they would understand if I refused the invitation. To share in their joy would be hard, but I really wanted to be a part of it.

As I sat in the church watching the ceremony, I thought of Brad. What kind of girl would he have married? What would his children have been like? He would have been a good father because he loved children and was very patient with them. Fighting back the tears was difficult and though I was not a total success at it, at least I showed some control.

Between the endless dreams, the uncontrollable tears, and my outburst of anger, I thought for sure I was losing my mind. My family doctor put me on an antidepressant and sleeping pills. He told me I would be over these feelings in a few months and everything would get back to normal.

I felt that was the most ignorant thing I had ever heard anyone say. Normal included Brad being alive and well.

The antidepressant made me sleep all day. What little time I was awake, everything seemed to be in slow motion. The dreams were still with me and I still cried a lot, but the pain in my heart was not as sharp.

I began taking the pills on a hit-and-miss basis. If I was having a bad time, I would stay home from work and take the pills.

The depression and the feeling of hopelessness were getting to be more than I could stand. Though I lived alone, I had three constant companions: depression, food, and alcohol. I could hide the depression with a smile accompanied by brave and optimistic conversation. When I was alone, I overate. When I was with others, I drank. But I was always depressed and few people ever knew how truly depressed I was.

As is the case in many families, mine used food as a means to comfort and soothe emotional hurts. It's a wonder that I wasn't as big as a house the way I ate. This wasn't new behavior. I had often used this way of escape when my life was filled with emotional pain.

My social and business life seemed to be centered around alcohol. What I didn't know then was that alcohol is a depressant. The drinking made my depression worse. I had experienced depression when I was divorced, but nothing that could compare with this.

Chapter Two

Make the Pain Stop

One night, about three months after Brad's death, I stopped after work to have a drink with two of my agents. Robin and Donna were more than simply people with whom I worked; they were also close friends. I'd never been able to, as they say, "hold my liquor," and since Brad's death I couldn't hold it at all. Two drinks and I was intoxicated. This night was no exception, so I went home early.

Over the past few weeks my depression had increased to the point that I felt I couldn't stand it any longer.

I was well aware of the dangers of innocent-looking prescription drugs because I had been addicted to prescription diet pills when I was a teenager. I was told they were not addictive and I should not worry about taking them. (Years later it came to light that these pills were, in fact, addictive.) I kicked the habit without any help or support and it was very hard to do. Ever since then I had been opposed to taking medication of any kind—I didn't even like to take an aspirin.

I was deeply depressed, and the alcohol in my system made me feel even worse. Through my tear-filled eyes I saw the antidepressant and sleeping pills on the bathroom counter. My first thought was, "I can't take those, I've been drinking." My next thought was, "I don't care. I want to die anyway. I can't go on this way." I took two handfuls.

They were hard to swallow and I kept gagging on them. I had to stop the pain. After taking the pills, I wrote Steve a note. I told him that I loved him and that I knew he would understand. There was no thought of the terrible pain and burden I would be placing on him and the rest of my family.

I felt so weak and helpless. None of this makes any sense to me now, but at the time, being intoxicated and in so much emotional pain, it seemed okay. After writing the note, I went to bed.

However, remembering something at work which needed attention the next day, I sat up in bed and placed a call to the cocktail lounge, hoping to catch Robin or Donna before they left. Donna came to the phone and I told her what needed to be done. I explained that I wouldn't be in the office the next day because I was going to be out of town.

She did not believe my story and kept asking, "What's wrong? You don't sound right."

I could feel myself falling asleep, yet I could still hear the slur of my words. Finally, because of her unrelenting persistence, I confessed to what I'd done. She made no verbal response. There was only the dial tone of the disconnected call.

As I would later learn, Donna went to the table where Robin was waiting, picked up her handbag, and said, "Pat's taken an overdose of pills, let's go."

Without saying a word, Robin sprang to her feet and followed Donna out the door. They ran to the car. My apartment was only five minutes away. When they arrived, I could hear them at the locked door, but they sounded very far away. Within seconds I floated into a deep death-like sleep.

Frantically breaking a window, they entered and with the speed of lightning they had me in the bathroom. My head was hanging over the toilet bowl while Robin's fingers probed my throat to find just the right spot to induce vomiting.

These courageous friends took on the task of saving my life. Many times in the past, Robin had taken charge under such circumstances, when she was a registered nurse in the emergency room.

After taking my clothes off, and then their own, they entered the shower with me in tow. Throughout the night they walked me continuously, talked to me, and forced me to respond.

The next morning they were exhausted from lack of sleep and their horrifying experience. They called Jim, the mayor of a nearby city and someone I had been dating for over a year. They asked for his help.

Robin give Jim instructions on how to care for me. She and Donna took a well-earned rest. One of the three was at my side day and night over the next three or four days. They would let me sleep for an hour or so, then walk me and force me to eat and drink.

I have no memory of these events. When I awoke, the window had already been repaired and all the mess cleaned up as if no trauma had taken place.

These brave people had taken a tremendous risk for me and all I could feel was resentment and anger toward them. How dare they interfere with my life! They didn't understand the agony of my pain! Couldn't they see how hopeless my life was? Damn them! Damn them! They had no right to interfere like that! Not only did I think these things, I verbalized them. I shouted at them to "Leave me alone," but my words fell on deaf ears.

My poor family also took the brunt of this anger. My daughter-in-law, Jan, had had an uneasy feeling about my welfare. She dropped by the apartment to check on me and discovered what had happened.

Sometimes the wisdom of youth is greater than that of the more mature. This was certainly one of those times. Although she had been asked not to tell the family, she used her own good judgment and revealed the secret.

With Jan and the others I behaved in a rude and hostile manner. At times I couldn't even speak to them. I tried, but the words stuck in my throat. It felt as if there was a ball of iron caught in my windpipe.

When Mother called and asked if I would see her, I said, "No, I don't want to see anyone." Not sure how to help me, she came anyway. It must have been heartbreaking for her to look into her daughter's eyes and see them flash such anger.

The helplessness she felt showed in her face. I wanted to say words that would make her feel better, but they wouldn't come out.

Did she understand my anger was not with her, but rather with myself? My hatred was not of her or of my friends—I hated myself.

In the course of talking, my mother came up with the idea of sending me on a short cruise to Mexico. She was desperate to help me, and thought I didn't feel as if I had the energy for it, I finally agreed to the trip. The trip was pleasant, but it didn't ease my emotional pain or my longing for Brad.

I have truly been blessed with wonderful friends and a marvelous family. Today I'm grateful to them!

A few days after my "awakening," my friend Mary Jo took me to a psychologist she knew. I saw him twice a week for about one month. He didn't know much about grief and knew even less about suicide. In fairness to him, psychologists today are much better informed about these matters. Now it is understood that many people who are in grief feel suicidal in the second to sixth month after the death of a loved one. If the death was a suicide, the suicidal feelings will be even stronger.

What I needed was to be able to talk to someone who understood my feelings of hopelessness and not wanting to live. When I tried to share these feelings, I was told I didn't really feel that way, that I had so much to live for and should be grateful for what I had.

I knew what I should be grateful for, but it didn't seem to matter. All this did was confirm in my mind that I was going insane.

I had not only the pain of my son's death to contend with, but also my own financial insecurity. In 1982 I was 44 years old with no work experience. Divorced with no alimony. I had to agree to pay $27,000 worth of bills. I had no automobile and a house that was foreclosed on two months after the divorce. Those two years before Brad's death had not been any bed of roses, but I managed.

When Brad died, I owned two automobiles: a Cadillac that I had taken as a commission and an Oldsmobile. I owned my real estate brokerage, and the bills had been taken care of. I had over $3000 in the bank. The money I had saved wasn't very much, but I had worked hard to save it and I felt that I was going to make a success of my life.

However, my success died with Brad.

The commission from the sale of the house, which was owned by the bank, carried me for a few months. The country was in a recession and the real estate market was at a standstill. If the agent made one sale every two months, they were working hard to get it, and then it would take 60 to 90 days before they would receive any money.

A constant state of worry about finances became a way of life for me. All I could think about was Brad and my lack of money. Anger with myself, Brad, God, the economy, my former husband, and anything else I could think of was part of my daily routine.

The psychologist helped me to understand that my anger was a normal part of what I was going through. He also helped me to see that although my former husband and I had lived a financially affluent life, we had also lived an emotionally bankrupt one. His years of alcoholism and my years in the role of an enabler had taken a heavy toll on the entire family.

I started attending Al-Anon meetings, hoping to gain a better understanding of myself and my former life. When I would speak of Brad's death at these meetings, people were sympathetic, but they couldn't relate to what I was feeling. I didn't want sympathy. I wanted to understand what had happened. Most of all I wanted Brad back.

I didn't have the energy or the money to find the help I needed. When I did speak with psychologists, who I thought could help me, I was disappointed. For the most part, their attitude toward me changed once they heard the word suicide. This reaction was something I was becoming accustomed to, not only from health-care professionals but from other people as well.

It was amazing how many people offered an unsolicited opinion about suicide when they didn't have personal or professional experience with it. Some acted as if they were angry with me, others would look at me with disgust, and others would hang their head so as not to look at me. I felt an overpowering sense of shame when people reacted to me in this manner. My close friends also became aware of this behavior toward me and they made every effort to protect me.

It would be years before I found the information which explained this behavior. All I knew was that I felt as if I were losing my mind.

Common sense told me that my son was not the only person to have died in this manner, but trying to find a support group pertaining to suicide was fruitless. I now know that suicide occurs about 85 times a day in this country. This means there are at least 500 new "survivors" left behind each day—family members and friends who have lost a loved one to suicide. Where were the other people who were grieving?

First Year

Brad died on February 19, 1984. He would have been 19 on March 21 of that year.

I stayed in bed most of the day on his birthday. My heart felt as if it would break with pain. How could I possibly go on without him?

On past birthdays I would, as most mothers do, think of the day he was born and about how small and sweet he was. I recalled all the cute things he did. The first time he smiled, his first unsteady steps, his chubby little legs, the way he sucked the two middle fingers of his right hand. Then, as he grew a little older, how proud he was when he learned to ride a bike, and how grown-up he felt on his first day of school.

The very memories which had brought me so much happiness in the past now brought me only more pain. Brad had held me in his arms many times. Sometimes in a playful way, restricting my movement, and other times in a gentle, loving way. He had a special tone in his voice when he would say, "I love you, Mom."

On this day, his birthday, I could feel his arms around me and hear his voice. I could smell the shampoo he used on his hair. I could feel the little stubble of beard on his cheek. Oh, how I longed for my baby!

That first year was filled with many small and large hurts. The most unexpected things would bring pain.

At Easter, Jan brought my grandson by to see me. He was holding a small stuffed bunny, which in turn was holding a little basket that held an Easter egg. My grandson looked up at me with that wide-eyed wonderment and excitement only a child can have. As he extended his little hand, offering me the bunny, I started to cry. I took Karl in my arms and held him so close he wiggled to get away.

Jan is a very compassionate person, and was understanding. No matter what she said or did, I couldn't stop crying. I felt so foolish. Instead of seeing my grandson, Karl, standing there, I was seeing Brad as a child.

At first I would go out of my way to keep from passing the schools Brad had attended. One day, while someone else was driving, we were on the street in front of the high school before I realized where we were. It was late afternoon and the students were all over the place. My companion and I had been talking, laughing, and having a good time. As I looked up from the magazine I had been reading to her, I thought I saw Brad. My heart leaped with excitement. Then reality set in and I bit my lip to keep from screaming.

With tears rolling down my face, I told myself that, from then on, I would never avoid any of the things or places which reminded me of Brad.

It was not only the local area that caused memories of Brad. My friend Jim often traveled to Sacramento on business. He was a kind and thoughtful man. He felt it would be good for me to get away from all the memories our area held, so he asked me if I would like to accompany him on his trip.

I welcomed the opportunity for a change of environment. At first this change seemed to be helping. By the end of the day, I was feeling a little better.

That evening Jim and I were to meet in the lobby of the hotel on our way to dinner. Standing alone in the elevator, I watched the panel light up as it indicated each floor in my descent to the lobby. Taking advantage of the few seconds delay before the doors of the elevator opened, I looked down to make one last adjustment of my clothing.

As the doors slowly opened, I looked up to see the lobby filled with young people dressed in formal attire. It was prom night! Unable to move, my mind raced back in time to Brad's prom night. How handsome he had looked in his white dinner jacket, with a pink rose boutonniere pinned to the lapel.

A feeling of guilt swept over me. Why hadn't I been of more help to him in his preparation for that event? Just as the doors started to close, Jim stepped between them. He took me by the hand and said, "Don't worry. We'll be having dinner with the senator and some other people in a private dining room." Without saying a word, I let him lead me to our destination. The others had already arrived and were seated. As I looked around the room, I smiled and prayed no one could see the guilt I felt.

This first year was like a rebirth in the respect that I was starting over. I was experiencing so many things for the first time, or for the first time without Brad.

We have all been asked the question, how many children do you have?, and we give our answer automatically.

The first time I was asked this after Brad's death, I wasn't sure how to answer. In my heart I had and will always have two children, but now I only had one in the physical sense. It was like being given a test I hadn't studied for. Today my answer to that question is: I have two children; one is living. Or sometimes I say: I have two children; one is deceased.

My mood swings were extreme all that year. Sometimes I would know what caused the change of mood, other times I wouldn't have a clue. I could be feeling good and something would remind me of

Brad. It might be something someone said, or something I might see, or even a smell which made me think of him.

For the benefit of the people who encountered me, I should have worn a sign like you see on the back of large trucks which say, 'Caution Wide Turns.' Mine should have said, 'Caution Wide Mood Swings.'

Thanksgiving and Christmas the year before had been extremely sad because of my father's death in October, but this year was unbearable.

My younger sister, Carol, is my only sibling. When we were children it was, I felt, my responsibility to protect her. This feeling of being responsible for her welfare was still a part of me. She had a heart attack in the early part of November. Once again, someone I loved was in pain and I couldn't protect them. She didn't look or feel well. We were all very concerned about her.

Carol was lying on the sofa as mother and I prepared the Thanksgiving dinner. We went about our task with hearts that were heavy from our sadness. There was little of the joking and laughter which had always been a part of our family.

Steve was still stationed in Turkey. I worried about him being alone in his grief, and I missed him. He is the strong silent type, with deep emotions that are difficult at times for him to verbalize. When he was home for Brad's funeral he had helped me in every way he knew how. Not only did he tell me in words, he also let me know he loved me in many large and small ways.

Steve had always been an exceptional person, planning for a military career since he was a small child.

While in high school, it was necessary for him to have surgery on his knee. I'll never forget the heart-breaking words of the surgeon: "You had better see to it this boy gets a good education because he'll never be able to climb telephone poles for a living. The good news is you'll never have to send him to war because he will be classified 4F."

How does one relay this kind of disappointing news to one's child? I asked the doctor not to tell Steve, saying I would do it.

The first few days after his return home, I struggled with how to tell him. Straightforward, right out with it was the only way I knew. After telling him, word for word, what the doctor had said, I suggested he start thinking of a different career. The look on his face was one of disbelief.

"Give me some time to think about what you've told me and then we'll discuss it," he said.

I had placed a small bell on his nightstand so that he could summon me when he had a need. No more than 15 minutes had passed when I heard the bell frantically ringing.

"Sit down, Mother, I want to talk to you," he said as I entered. I sat on his bed as he continued to speak.

"You have always told me I could have anything I want if I work hard and keep my goal in mind. Now, the first time I face a real obstacle you are telling me I can't have what I want."

"Steve, some things in life are physically impossible and we must accept them."

"That may be true, but this is not one of them."

He was overjoyed when in his senior year of high school he received word that he had an appointment to the military academy West Point. This was an honor he had worked hard to achieve. It was terribly disappointing when he failed the physical because of his knee.

With his determination, he was not to be stopped. His first year of college he attempted to join the R.O.T.C. The knee once again became an issue.

He argued and fought with the army until someone agreed that they would accept him if he could obtain a letter from his doctor stating he was physically sound. The surgeon would not give him such a letter, so he obtained one from our family doctor. At long last he had what he wanted most. He was in the army!

Doing outstandingly well, he graduated from college and R.O.T.C. with honors. We were all extremely proud of him. Brad was especially proud of his big brother and wanted to be just like him.

Steve was now far from home and the people who loved him, enduring the pain of grief for his grandfather and little brother, alone in a foreign land.

The holidays are an extremely difficult time for people who are grieving. We all need the support of friends and family at a time like this.

That's one of the many reasons I was so upset when, years later, I was informed of a letter Larry had sent to Steve, while he was in Turkey, saying he felt Steve was responsible for Brad's death. It is not uncommon for people to attempt to place blame after a death, and especially when the death is by suicide, but of course there was no truth to this accusation. Steve and Jan had protected me from that hurt, as they had so many other hurts.

The family had chosen not to burden Steve with the fact that I had made an attempt at suicide. A few weeks after the attempt, I called Steve and asked if he would agree to my trying to get him stationed stateside. He agreed with my idea. I had been in touch with my congressman, asking for his help.

Steve was not home in time for that first Thanksgiving without Brad.

Christmas

Thanksgiving had come and gone like a dark cloud on a cold winter day. We had all, somehow, managed to survive it. Now we had another hurdle to get past: Christmas. This time of year was very special to our family, as it is to most. We were lavish gift-givers and it had always been fun to select just the right gift for each person. This year there was no fun in the shopping. Everything I saw was another reminder of Brad.

How could we possibly go on with "business as usual?" Family tradition seemed so frivolous and unimportant. All I could think of was the description of the events preceding Brad's death, which his father told me the day of the funeral.

He said he had accused Brad of taking his watch. Brad told his father he had not seen the watch. As they argued, Larry threw Brad against the wall, holding him there and shouting at him. Brad didn't fight back. Larry left the house, telling Brad he should think about what he had done.

Upon his return, about one hour later, he found a puppy whining and scratching at the door to Brad's bedroom. Larry told me he felt angry again with Brad, because the puppy was in the house. Then he opened the door and found Brad's lifeless body lying on the blood-soaked bed.

That afternoon Larry found his watch lying in a field, where it had fallen from his wrist when the clasp had broken.

Why, oh why, did he find it necessary to tell me these things? This picture of my son on his deathbed and those events were more than I could stand. They stayed with me night and day. How could I go on living with this heartache? How could I ever deal with the anger I felt not only toward Larry, but toward myself as well?

The only ray of sunshine was in the fact that Steve would be home for Christmas. In his usual capable way, he had taken over when the congressman had failed. Through his own efforts, he would now be stationed less than three hours from where I lived. What a wonderful Christmas gift this was to us all.

At this point some acquaintances of mine were starting to become impatient with me, saying things like, "It's been 10 months now, don't you think it's time to get on with your life?" or, "Let go of the past." These people meant well; they just didn't have any idea what I was going through. My close friends never let me down. Even though they didn't always understand, they always had empathy and compassion.

No one could have been more impatient with me than I was with myself. I had gained 15 pounds and was not happy with the way I looked. Although I was always well-groomed, I looked tired all the time. There was a good reason for this—I was!

I hadn't slept well in 10 months. Falling asleep was difficult. Once sleep came, the dreams of Brad would also come.

When I awoke from these dreams, I didn't want to go back to sleep for fear they would start once more. They were so real I would awake to the sound of my own screams. Each morning, in those first few seconds after awakening, I wouldn't remember that Brad was dead. Then reality would hit me full force, and the pain was as though I were hearing for the first time those shocking words, "Pat, Brad is dead."

For 10 months I hadn't been able to relax. I was always on edge, with muscles as taut as steel bands. My teeth would ache from the pressure of being clamped together. Some part of my body was always in motion, either slight or extreme. A foot moving back and forth, a finger tapping, or wringing my hands. I'd been working with some relaxation exercises without a great deal of success.

One night, not too long before Christmas, while doing a relaxation exercise, I became aware that my body was perfectly still, and had been for about five minutes. It was a wonderful feeling. Then a thought of Brad crossed my mind and I started to become tense again. At least now I knew what the feeling was like, which meant I could reproduce it, if I just kept working at it. Concentration was extremely difficult, but I knew that I must not give up.

By the time Christmas Eve arrived, not even the joy of having Steve home could lift my spirits. My heartache and longing for Brad was all consuming.

Our small family gathered at my mother's home, which was our custom on Christmas Eve. The buffet menu was the same as it had been for years, with all our favorite foods. We all looked forward to Mother's wonderful pecan pie.

The table was beautifully set with a large centerpiece of fresh red and white carnations, sprigs of evergreen, small pine cones, and little red and green balls. Flickering candlelight danced off the gleaming silver and crystal with which the table had been set.

The tree was in the same corner of the living room with the same ornaments hanging from its branches, as it was every year. As always, an abundance of carefully wrapped gifts lay under and around the tree.

Things may have looked the same, but, oh how they had changed. Daddy was not sitting in his large overstuffed chair, hooked to his lifeline of oxygen, with Brad sitting nearby inquiring, "How do you feel tonight, Granddad?" He would then tell him some dumb joke because he wasn't sure of what else to say.

Yes, the important things had changed. It was difficult for me to accept the fact that Brad would not be walking through the back door at any minute.

I had watched my father die and had seen him in his coffin, so I could accept his death as reality. But with Brad it was different. Not only had I not seen his body after death, I had not seen him for more than a month before the death. The only real confirmation I had that he was in fact dead was the death certificate. A piece of paper, that's all I had. Almost 19 years of loving and caring for this child and now a piece of paper was all I had to confirm his death, and it held that horrible word "suicide."

Once again I accepted all these feelings as more evidence that I was losing my mind. Through education, I now understand that viewing the body, although it is very painful at the time, helps one to accept the death as reality.

Of all the gifts I received that Christmas, I can remember only one. This gift, which was given to me by my niece Tracy, was a simple one that was to set me on a course of self-understanding, for which I will be forever grateful.

From the size and feel of the package, I could tell there was a book inside. All the family was aware I enjoy reading, so it was not unusual for them to give me books. But this year I wasn't excited about receiving one. It was very difficult for me to concentrate on reading, or anything else for that matter. Removing the paper, I was surprised to find the book was clothbound. It had a soft pink background with tiny rosebuds which were white. Opening it, I found blank pages. A journal! Thanking Tracy, I said, "I've never kept a journal, but I'll start on this one tonight."

When I arrived back at my apartment, it was dark, with a chill in the air. I gathered up as many gifts as I could carry at one time and locked the car. In my struggle to unlock the apartment door, I dropped the journal. My little home was warm and inviting, and I chose to leave the remainder of the gifts in the car until morning. As I slipped into bed, I remembered the journal was still outside. I retrieved it, and as I sat on the bed, I thought "How does one go about this? I guess it doesn't matter, no one will ever see it."

The first thing I wrote was:

> *December 24, 1984—From Tracy.*

Staring at the blank page for a few minutes I finally wrote:

> *12-24-84. All the family is together tonight. I miss Brad and Daddy more than ever. Cried most of the night.*

Although these few words were a pathetic attempt at expressing my emotions, they were a start. Some days I couldn't do any more than write one word—"DEPRESSED." Disciplining myself to write in the journal was a task. Each day I would write something, but I found it difficult to write about Brad.

> *12-25-84. Still crying off and on. I miss Brad so much. How I wished I could have helped him. I feel cheated of all that should have been.*

I had underlined the word "should." Every hour of each day Brad was in my thoughts, and yet I didn't write about him again until two weeks later.

> *1-7-85. Been crying—missing Brad, I miss him so much. When is life going to quit being such a bummer? Carol is in the hospital for the test on her heart. This family has had about all it can take. Oh, God, please help our lives to get better soon.*

After making an entry I would have a feeling of relief. There were days when I felt this journal was my only confirmation that I was alive. Years later, while attending a grief recovery class at Loma Linda University Medical Center, I learned that journal-keeping is recommended as a part of good grief recovery. A journal is an important part of my life now. I continue to keep one.

Afraid

Football and boxing are sports I've always felt have a degree of violence, but I've enjoyed them anyway. Detective stories, murder mysteries, and war movies all have some degree of violence in them, but I've also enjoyed being entertained by these things.

After Brad's death, I couldn't bear to read or watch any form of violence, no matter how slight. Even to see one person push another in an aggressive manner was upsetting. To witness an argument was painful. The sight of a gun would cause my palms to sweat and my muscles to become tight. Needless to say, feeling as I did, television wasn't one of my favorite ways to pass time, and reading the daily newspaper a real task.

In the past, I had usually been able to keep my wits about myself when faced with a tense situation. That had changed.

While standing in my office one day, looking out the window, a pick-up truck came speeding up the street and stopped in the street. Following close behind the truck was a small white car, which also came to a sudden stop. A young man about 20 years of age jumped from the pickup, and another from the car. They were shouting profanities at each other. The young man with the truck reached into the back of it and brought out a pool cue. He started beating the other young man with it. The man being attacked tried to fight off his assailant. Blood was all over their clothes as they fell to the ground.

With a similar situation in the past, I felt concern and excitement, went to the phone, called the police, and reported what was happening. Then I took down the license number of each vehicle.

Instead of doing this, I became hysterical; tears filled my eyes as I screamed at the agents to call the police. My heart was pounding, my palms sweating. In my mind, that was Brad out there in the street being attacked. I had to help him! As I started to run out the door, one of the agents stopped me. I was shaking and tried to gain my composure. I made no sense in the things I was saying.

Living alone or being alone were things I'd never been afraid of. If I heard a noise at night, I would investigate it. Once I assured myself everything was all right, I would forget about it. Now I was aware of every little noise.

Late one night, after having spent the day on a boat, far out on the Pacific Ocean, I received a telephone call from a man who was threatening me with harm. He said he knew where I lived and he had been following me all day. Having spent the day as I had, there was no way he could have been following me. Before Brad's death, I would've simply hung up the telephone and forgotten the whole thing. But now it frightened me. It didn't matter that logically there was no way he could have followed me—I called the police anyway. It didn't take more than 15 minutes for the officer to arrive, but by the time he got there I was extremely upset.

Afraid to turn on a light, I sat alone in the dark watching the door and windows, listening for the sound of footsteps. When the doorbell rang, I jumped to my feet and said with what I hoped was a calm voice, "Who is it?" That officer looked like a guardian angel, standing there in his blue uniform. He took the report, then told me this man had been calling other people at random saying the same thing. After he left, I was still upset and had a very restless night.

My fear was not only for my own safety, but others as well. I had an unrealistic need to know where my family members were at all times. A feeling of fear came over me every time the telephone rang. I felt that if I answered it someone would tell me bad news. This unnecessary fear of everything lasted for about one and a half years, although at times I still hesitate to answer the telephone.

Today, I still don't like to witness violence, but I don't become hysterical over it. Football and boxing are once again enjoyable, but not as much as they once were.

Second Year

With Thanksgiving and Christmas out of the way, I dreaded the approach of February 19th, the anniversary date of Brad's death, and then his birthday on March 21st. There had to be something I could do to make these dates less painful.

Now that it had been almost one year since his death, I no longer thought of him every second of the day. The thoughts now came every 30 minutes or so; sometimes even an hour would pass without a thought of him. The first time I realized this had happened, I felt guilty about it, as if I were being disloyal to him in some way.

Although I had close friends who were willing to listen to me talk about Brad and his death, I couldn't do much of it. I could talk about my anger, but that's where it would stop. My dear friend, Mary Jo, would try to get me to open up to her, but I would just become upset with her.

Other people could see what I was doing to myself, but I couldn't. I didn't want anyone to see how weak and helpless I felt. As long as there were other people around, I would talk brave and try to act as if nothing had happened that I couldn't handle just fine by myself. My heart was breaking and I couldn't let anyone see it. I would cover my pain with laughter and jokes. How alike Brad and I were.

We talked a lot in our family, but we didn't know how to communicate our feelings. We would hold our feelings inside and talk around them, but never about them. We never ever talked about what hurt. It wasn't that we didn't want to, we didn't know how to express these feelings in words.

Our family motto seemed to be "Don't talk about the things that hurt and they will go away." How wrong we were! It would be years before I learned how to talk about feelings and the pain they can often bring.

It was almost one year before I could bring myself to visit the mausoleum where Brad's ashes and my father's body were interred. I didn't want to make this visit, but felt I had to do it. Mary Jo went with me for support.

As I stood there looking up at his name carved in the cold, hard marble, I wanted to scream, "No, no, my baby is not dead." The tears streamed down my face. My knees felt weak. Why did this have to be true? Why couldn't I wake up from this terrible dream? "I want my baby back." "Oh, God, please let me have another chance. I'll be a better mother. Please God, oh please." There of course was no answer to my cries. No miracle was found that day or any other, only the pain, the never-ending pain.

The anniversary date of his death was drawing near and I knew I must do something to keep myself busy. Business had been better and I had a little extra money, so I registered for a seminar on real estate law and taxation, which was to be held in Palm Springs, California.

My friend Robin and I drove to, as some say, "The Springs." The hotel where we stayed was beautiful, and the warm desert air felt good. This will be just what the doctor ordered, I thought. Three days in a peaceful setting will help. And it did the first day.

The seminar was to start early the next morning, so Robin and I drove around the city enjoying the sights. It seemed like absolute madness that life was going on without Brad. I felt so empty and useless. Why had his life been short and so very sad? Why was I still living when my life had no purpose or meaning? These were my thoughts as we drove, but I couldn't talk about them.

After having an early dinner, we sat in our suite of rooms. The hotel was the type where all the accommodations are suites, with one bedroom, a living room, and a small kitchen. It was a new hotel, so everything was shiny clean.

We sat in this pleasant atmosphere having an after-dinner drink and talked about real estate and our personal lives. Being sure to stay away from the topic of Brad's death, we chose to lament the relationships we were involved in.

The next day was the day before the anniversary. It was also the legal portion of the seminar. Real estate law had always been easy for me to understand, so even though it was hard for me to concentrate, I did well in the class.

The next day was a different story! I didn't sleep well that night, having dreams of Brad all night long. Of course this prevented my friend from sleeping as well. We finally got out of our beds and talked most of the night. She understood I was having a difficult time. We talked about a lot of things that night, but very little about Brad.

It seemed we had just fallen asleep when the alarm clock made its harsh sound, informing us it was time to start our day. The day I had lived in dread of had arrived. My eyes were red and swollen and my thoughts were utter confusion as I entered the classroom. Taxation was a subject I had trouble with under the best of circumstances, so I knew this was not going to be easy.

The instructor had been very pleasant the day before, but now he seemed to be a demon with one objective, to drive me into the ground. As he addressed the more difficult questions to me, I would freeze. My mind became blank, totally void of the information he was looking for. Not only did I feel stupid, I looked stupid as well. His frustration with me became more obvious as the day wore on. At last he stood before me with his hands on his hips, looking down into my face, shouting, "I know that you understand the question. I'm not going to leave you alone until you give me the right answer." I could feel the tears coming into my eyes. "Please God, don't let these people see me cry" were my thoughts. I'll never know if the answer I gave was correct or if the instructor just gave up on me.

The drive home was a somber one. All I wanted was to be by myself so I could cry until I couldn't cry any more. I felt so humiliated and ashamed.

A few days later, I received a call from a young couple who had been referred to me because they had been trying, with no success, to sell their condominium. After taking a look at it, I could understand why they had been unsuccessful.

It was extremely clean and well-kept but in a poor neighborhood. Although the loan was less than desirable, it could be assumed without a buyer having to qualify.

I told the couple I would buy their condominium if they agreed to buy the new home they planned to purchase through me. This way I could use the money I earned from the sale to purchase their condominium. We made our agreement and everyone was happy. I found them a new home and our escrows were closed before Brad's birthday.

The condominium was small, with three bedrooms and two baths. It was not much of a place when compared with the large, lovely homes in the best of neighborhoods that I had lived in most of my life. But I felt such a sense of pride when I received the key. What a great feeling! At last, after three long years, once again I was the owner of my own home.

Moving into my little place, while putting things away, my thoughts were of Brad and how pleased he would be with me. These thoughts caused me to think of a box of pictures. I began looking for the box but couldn't find it. The longer I looked, the more panic I felt. The box contained every picture I owned of Brad. In my state of panic, I was throwing things out of the way as the search went on in vain. Finally, stopping from exhaustion, I sat with tears flowing down my face like cascading waterfalls. How careless of me! How stupid of me! Why hadn't I been more careful with something so valuable!

Then I saw the box where it had been placed with care out of harm's way. Although these pictures were extremely important to me, I couldn't bear the pain of looking at them and didn't do so until the next year.

On Brad's birthday, I chose to attend another seminar, but this time all I had to do was sit and listen. This was also about real estate, except it was how to get rich overnight.

We had been receiving a lot of calls from buyers wanting to purchase property with no money down. When times are hard economically, as they were then, these get-rich-quick schemes become popular. I felt I should be informed as to what people were being told, and it was a distraction from the thoughts of Brad, so I went to the seminar.

It was amazing to see hundreds of people being so gullible and spending hundreds of hard-earned dollars on the poorest of information. The good thing about all of this was it temporarily interrupted my thoughts of Brad.

The seminar had stimulated ideas on how I could train the agents in my office to make better use of the telephone. That night I made notes on how to set up a training program. For the first time in over a year, I could concentrate on something without having thoughts of Brad that were so overpowering I would have to stop working because of tears.

This was a wonderful feeling, but when I tried to sleep, the thoughts of Brad returned with full force. Once again I cried myself to sleep with a feeling of hopelessness. I was convinced these horrible feelings would be with me the rest of my life. But I also knew, even though I couldn't see any reason to go on living with this pain, I had no choice but to move forward with my life, one day at a time, as if serving a jail sentence.

Was this my punishment for being such a bad mother? I had done the best I knew how and it wasn't good enough. Oh, intellectually I knew this was not true, but emotionally I was not so sure.

Working with the agents on the new training program became the highlight of my week. Each meeting would start with a short pep talk from me on subjects like attitude, self-talk, and confidence. They seemed to enjoy the training and showed improvement in their work.

These talks probably helped me more than they did the agents. I could feel my self-confidence slowly returning. It was important to me that they not see how unhappy, insecure, and frightened of life I was.

After Brad's death, my self-confidence level had gone down to zero. I was afraid to do anything for fear of doing it wrong. This feeling had become stronger as the second year wore on.

In September I had an opportunity to travel to Europe for almost a month. No matter where I went, I felt Brad's presence very strongly. He was with me every step of the way. At first I tried to ignore this feeling, but it was so strong I gave in to it. As crazy as it must sound, I enjoyed feeling him near me.

I had this sense of his presence from time to time over the past year, but it brought a feeling of sadness and was never this strong, or lasted so long.

I could better understand this if we had planned a trip like this one at some point in time, but we had never talked of travelling to Europe together. Perhaps the trip was symbolic of me getting ready to let go of the past. I don't know that I will every really understand what happened, but I did enjoy the experience and the feeling I got from it. After returning home, the feeling left and everything seemed a little better somehow.

An experience like this is not uncommon, it turns out. Many people have a similar experience around the 16th to 24th month following the death. One young woman, who attends a suicide survivors support group which I facilitate, shared with us a dream she had in the 18th month after the suicide of her husband. There had not been a funeral for him and she had been unable to cry for many months, stating that she felt if the tears started they would never stop. The dream was of his funeral—it was vivid in every detail. The experience was extremely real and the pain almost unbearable. Her pillow was soaked with the tears she shed for her husband. Although this was a painful experience, she had a sense of release, of letting go, and could now shed the tears which help one to heal. This dream brought her comfort; she could face her grief.

Another case was a man whose wife had died by suicide. They owned a cabin in the mountains some 100 miles from where they lived. His wife had loved the cabin and he found himself unable to visit it. Although he was extremely depressed, 19 months after her death he felt an overpowering need to visit the cabin. The feeling of his wife's presence was with him night and day for the week he stayed there. Instead of it being frightening or upsetting the way it had been in the past, he found a sense of comfort in the experience. As he told me, they had a wonderful week together, and he was able to move on with his life from that point.

Not everyone has such a dramatic turning point, but for those of us who do, we will never cease to be amazed by it.

Chapter Three

My Story

The date was November 2, 1985. I had gone to bed feeling restless. This was the date Brad had been hit by a car when he was nine. A feeling of depression had been with me for days. I wanted to forget the past but couldn't. What could I do with these terrible memories?

After tossing and turning for hours, sleep finally came to me, though not for long. At 2 A.M. I awoke. Not wanting to be a prisoner of my thoughts, I got out of bed and went to the kitchen table where I had placed my briefcase the night before. I took out a legal pad and pen. This would be a good time to write. A few weeks earlier I had agreed to give a speech for Al-Anon. Why not work on it now?

Al-Anon is a support group for the families of alcoholics. They do a tremendous amount of good, but when I attended the meetings, I wanted to scream at the people, "Get out of these relationships before they destroy you and kill your children." Of course I never said this to anyone, because intellectually I understood this was only my truth, not theirs.

As I started to write, words and emotion poured from inside me. The tears were blinding, but I couldn't stop writing. It was as if I were bathing my soul in my own tears.

This is what came out:

> *Hi! My name is Pat and I would like to share my story with you.*
>
> *I was married to an alcoholic for 18 years. I now realize that I lived in a state of fear for most of my life. Fear is what kept me in that marriage, as well as my feelings of responsibility. Boy, you wouldn't believe how responsible*

I felt. You would, but the rest of the world couldn't even start to understand. The more fear I had, the less self-esteem I had. The less self-esteem I had, the more fear I had. And so it went, around and around, just like a toy top spinning. The only way it will stop is to run down or fall over. I had run down years before I got the courage to do something different with my life.

How did I gain the courage? Who really knows? I think it was a combination of things. For one, I just couldn't take life the way it was, and of course, I had read all those self-help books. You should have seen all those books, everything from Pulling Your Own Strings *by Dr. Dryer to* Stop Running Scared *by Dr. Fensterheim. For years I just knew something had to be wrong with me.*

After all, I was responsible for everything—my husband's drinking, my parent's health, my children, if they did anything wrong, for family finances, the dogs, the mailman, the weather, etc. You name it and I could find a way to be responsible for it. Oh! I wasn't so arrogant as to feel responsible for their origination, only for their well-being. I was the one to see to it that their lives went well. Being responsible the way I was, I had to be strong. I could take anything, absolutely anything at all. I knew this was true because everyone told me so, which made me feel responsible to be stronger.

Boy! What a problem. Fear set in, fear that someone might find out that I was not as strong as everyone believed. What if I let someone down? With each new fear my self-esteem would drop, and as my self-esteem became lower and lower, the fears became higher and higher.

Fear that I would make a mistake, and of course, that which you fear the most will come about, and it did. In my mind everything I did was a mistake; I became my own enemy. I was too fat. I never wore the right clothes.

If I had a broken fingernail, I didn't want to go out of the house, because someone might see it and find fault with me. God knows I couldn't stand for anyone to find fault with me because I had already found it all by myself.

You see, I had this big, big job of covering up so no one would know that a loser I really was. The more I found wrong with myself, the more I wanted to be perfect and everyone around me to be perfect. It just wasn't there, and it couldn't be done. Now I know it's okay not to be perfect.

It has taken four long years to learn these and many more things about myself. What an education it's been! I feel as if I've earned my Ph.D in life!

The first part of education was being married to an alcoholic for so many years. This was a daily class on how to stand my ground in a fight, how to negotiate, how to listen so intently that you became void of emotion. How to lie for him and cover up your disgrace, and then how not to lie for him because you start to understand that it is not your disgrace. To learn that you're not responsible for his actions. In this class you eventually learn what the children have known for years, that their father is an alcoholic. Even in the years you tried to cover it up, they knew.

You learn that the children don't like him because he has belittled and embarrassed them so often. You learn your parents don't like him because of the way he has treated you and the children. You also learn the rest of the world thinks he is a real good guy. After all, they see him as always happy and buying drinks for everyone.

The next class I took was Illness. In this class I learned how to care for my nine-year-old son after he had been hit by a car while crossing the street. He was in a coma for 30 days; I learned to wait, hope, and pray. When he came home from the hospital, I learned how to care for a child who was paralyzed on the right side of his body and the left side of his face. I became the teacher. I taught him the things he had known only 30 days before, how to feed himself, how to button his shirt, how to walk and talk. And I learned. Boy, did I learn! I learned what dedication is, and I learned what true courage is in a little boy facing the world with such a large burden. What courage it took to go on when the other children made fun of him. What courage it took to go on when he was in pain. Oh yes, I learned so much in this class, with a little nine-year-old teacher.

Then came the class in Divorce and along with this class I got extra credit for financial failure. Not only did I get to start over again. I got to do it broke. Not your average broke, but in the hole.

We had just finished building a very expensive home. My ex-husband had "borrowed" a lot of money from the construction loan, which meant the subcontractors could not be paid. I took on all the debts. I really wanted out, and after all I was superwoman! I'd find a way. No car, no money, no job, and no work experience, but I would find a way to make it work. Well, the house was eventually repossessed, but I did find a way to hold my life together and keep on going.

In this class I learned what it was like to be scared, scared like I had never been before. I learned not to answer the phone because it could be someone wanting the money owed to them (which I didn't have). I learned to hate! I learned the embarrassment of a friend's husband trying to seduce me. I learned to be tough and hard. I learned to be alone and lonely (I had already learned to be lonely when I was married). I learned what it is like to have people pity me, which I hate. I learned what it is like to drink too much for days on end. I learned true depression. I learned to stand on my own and take care of myself.

The next class was How To Run Your Own Business. I opened a real estate company when interest rates were at an all-time high of 19% and 20%. I learned to deal with the state and attorneys. I learned to be a leader, I learned to deal with employees, I learned to hire and dismiss people. I learned to make fast decisions and stand by them. I learned to stand on my own. I learned to take care of myself and others.

The next class was in Death. First my father, who had a very long illness. I had always loved my mother, but now I learned to like and respect her for taking care of him. I learned that I don't want to be old and sick and take so long to die. I learned to miss my Daddy.

Then three months later, my son, who had been so brave when he was nine, shot himself to death when he was 18 years of age. I learned what true sorrow is. I learned how your arms can ache to hold your baby just once more. I learned that people do care and want to help. I learned depression so deep that I tried to take my own life, and I learned about God's Will.

The next class I took was on Living. All the other classes were a prerequisite for this one. In this class I learned that life will go on, in fact, must go on. I learned that to truly take part in life is living. The hurting is just as much a part of living as the joys are.

This class has taught me to find joy in the small things of life, like a sunny day, a kitten at play, a child's warm smile, and an older person's spunk. Yes, this class has taught me to be grateful. Grateful for my remaining son, whom I love and adore. I'm so very proud of him and his family, his wonderful wife, and my delightful grandchildren.

Living is looking at what I have, not at what was or what I've lost. Living is a true appreciation for family, good friends, and honest work.

> *Then came the class on Understanding and Enlightenment. What a wonderful and sometimes confusing class this is. In this class you start to find the answers to some of the "Whys" you've been asking over the years. Like when I cried out in my anguish and asked: "Why me God? Why so much tragedy in my life? Why not give some of it to the other guy?"*
>
> *It was in this class that I came to understand life is a journey of learning. Each individual life has it share of tragedy and glory. We must each follow our own path to fulfillment and happiness.*
>
> *If my story has helped you in any small way, I am pleased, for I have accomplished my goal.*

By the time I had finished writing this speech for Al-Anon, I'd gone through two boxes of tissue. These tears were very therapeutic. This was a real attempt at facing the issues and feelings which were bothering me—an attempt at being honest with myself. Even as I was writing the part about "Why me God?" I could feel myself becoming aware that my life was at this place because of the choices I had made, not because of some outside force doing it for or to me. The idea of helping other people to understand was appealing, though I didn't have enough understanding myself to be of any real help to anyone else at that point in time.

I have had more tragedy in my life than some people have, but also far, far less than so many others have.

I chose not to give this speech to Al-Anon, but did present it one time at a church. For weeks, I read and reread this story, crying each time. When my family read it, they were all amazed, saying, "I had no idea you felt this way; you have always been so strong." What relief, at long last, to have these feelings of mine be known.

About a year later, while attending a class at the University of California, I learned that this writing process is recommend as a tool to help patients in psychotherapy.

We all have a very special story to tell and that is the story of our own life. When it is written out, we can see it more clearly and look at it in an objective manner. Some recommend starting with the earliest memories and moving forward in time to the present. Although I didn't do this, I still found the writing to be extremely helpful.

Understanding

With this little drop of understanding came a thirst for more knowledge. The first psychologist I had seen after Brad's death told me, "Many people build a brick wall around their emotions in an attempt at self-protection. As a doctor, I can remove these bricks one at a time. You have built a wall of iron and it will never come down. I know this because every time I ask you a question that requires an emotional response, you give me an intellectual answer."

His words bothered me and kept echoing in my mind. I wasn't sure what he meant. Was he saying I was a hopeless case? After going through the pain of writing "my story," I could see it was going to take a lot of work for me to have better self-understanding, but I could also see that I was not a hopeless case. This wall-building had started in early childhood, as it does with most of us. If the wall needed to come down, I was ready, and would find a way to accomplish the task.

Drinking had become a thing of the past for some months and I was also getting much butter at relaxing my body. The psychology department of bookstores became my favorite place to shop. Books about suicide were never on the shelf and I was too ashamed to ask for them.

Believing I had truly gone over the edge of sanity, it became my mission to find a way back. Every night I would read until the wee hours of the morning. Books on self-esteem, saying no, self-confidence, relationships, psychology of selling, and books on having it all were all over my home. My Bible was always open to some passage I had been reading in search of answers. But not one book on grief was among the lot. It never dawned on me that what I was feeling could be grief and therefore quite normal. One book that did help me was *Feeling Good* by David D. Burns, M.D.—a self-help book on depression.

For months I didn't have much of a social life because all I wanted to do was read and listen to motivational tapes. My friends were starting to become concerned about my being alone so much of the time. How could I explain to them that I felt as if I were fighting for my very life? Would they understand these horrible fears I was living with? How shocked they would have been to know the truth about me. Acting as if nothing was wrong became harder with each passing day, but so far my secret was safe.

Unbeknown to me, my accountant had an extreme cocaine habit. The I:R.S. decided to audit all of his clients. He handled both my personal and business taxes, so of course they paid me a visit. The stress of having them in my office every day for two weeks was a terrible experience.

The end result was that I owed them what was to me a tremendous amount of money. Now I had an unrealistic feeling of having failed at business. Couldn't I do anything right? This new worry was one I never expected to be confronted with. My nightly dreams of Brad were interwoven with monsters and violence. I felt so defeated and beat down.

Self-doubt, unrealistic feelings, extreme fatigue (mental and physical), relentless dreams of the deceased, and withdrawal are all part of the feelings and behavior of grief. If a person has self-doubt and insecurities, as I did, before the death, the feelings will become exaggerated after the loss of a loved one.

At this point I would have made a deal with the devil himself to get out from under all the pressure I was feeling. Why couldn't I get my life on track? How would I ever get the money to pay the back taxes? Would this longing for Brad ever stop? Would the part of my heart which had been ripped away ever mend? Was depression to be a way of life for me?

The second Christmas without Brad was fast approaching and I didn't feel as if I could make it through the pain. Christmas Eve at my mother's home was the same as always and much to my surprise it was not nearly as painful as it had been the year before. We all had a sense of sadness from missing Brad and Daddy, but it wasn't as gut-wrenching as last year.

Christmas Day was spent with Steve and his family.

On 12-27-85 I wrote in my journal:

> *Went out to Steve & Jan's for Christmas, stayed overnight, and it was so very nice. Jan is very sweet and Steve is always my good boy. I love them all so much, the boys are wonderful. I'm feeling better.*

If I had been able to write about Brad I would have felt better yet. Suppressing my emotions was the only way I knew to handle them. If the family had been more open, and each of us had talked about our feelings, we would have helped each other. Oh, we tried, but when someone would bring up Brad or Daddy, we would talk about something they did or said, but we were careful not to express how we felt, other than to say we missed them.

From that standpoint, this Christmas Day was different because I had made a tape of "my story" and the family listened to it. This helped us all to talk about our feelings in a more direct manner. Even with the help of the tape, Steve and I were still the ones who had the most difficulty expressing our feelings. This was the first time we collectively discussed our anger, bitterness, and sadness, and our feelings that an injustice had been done.

Darkest Before Dawn

Sometimes it seems things have to get worse before they can improve. This new year wasn't getting off to a very good start. The I.R.S. was demanding money. My former husband was once again taking me to court in an attempt to obtain money from me. One of my agents had made a mistake in a transaction and the real estate commissioner was coming down on me. Plus my house payment had gone up.

I felt as if a pack of wild dogs were tearing me apart; it was hard to keep going. Each day seemed to be a new test of my courage to face life.

To bring some financial relief from the higher house payment, I decided to rent out one of the bedrooms. Within a couple of days, I had found what I thought was the right person, a man Jim had introduced to me.

He was married and lived in another state, but business brought him to our city. Being in and out of the area over the last year or so, he was well-known and liked. While the three of us were having lunch one day, he said he was tired of living in a hotel and was only in town two weeks out of the month. We made an agreement that he would rent the room. He wanted to move in that day, which was fine with me—the sooner I could get the money, the better.

The first week was great. We didn't see much of each other because of the hours we worked. By the second week, I knew what a mistake I had made. He had a drinking problem and was a very messy person in the home. He would leave the doors unlocked, so I worried about the possibility of a robbery. I felt a need to lock my bedroom door. There was no longer a sense of freedom or safety in my own home. How angry I was to be in this position, but I suppressed the anger because of my need for money. The real estate market was still slow, but I was able to complete some transactions.

My relationship with Jim was changing too. It seemed that we couldn't be together more than a few minutes without a disagreement or a full-blown argument. We couldn't agree on much of anything. Our relationship had always been a stormy one. I didn't want any kind of commitment, and for over two years he had been wanting me to marry him. He was a good man and very kind to me. Jim would be a fine husband for someone. I just didn't want that someone to be me. We were slowly spending less time together.

Between my grief for Brad and all the other pressures, I felt like a zombie. It was hard for me to get out of bed in the mornings and I had a very difficult time going to sleep at night. Living in fear was causing me extreme stress and anxiety.

The one bright spot during this time was Gene. He had come into my life about two weeks before I rented the room. Gene had his own troubles. He was being divorced. His 83-year-old mother, who had Alzheimer's disease, lived with him. His business was not doing well.

The old saying "misery loves company" held true with us. When we were together, our troubles seemed to lessen. He had an almost childlike curiosity about everything and was very open with his feelings. Because of his openness, he saw nothing wrong with the probing questions he asked about Brad. At times I felt resentment for his intrusion. On other occasions, when he would say, "I want to know Brad; will you please share him with me?" it felt better. But it hurt to answer the questions he asked, so I gave him brief answers.

The townhouse he lived in was in a complex that had security gates, so visitors had to call in from a phone at the gate before they were allowed in. A feeling of safety would come over me as I passed through these gates—it was a place to hide out. The telephone number was unlisted, and I wouldn't tell anyone where I was or give out the phone number.

I had the feeling that I didn't exist while in this safe haven. More and more of my time was spent behind these gates. They couldn't stop my dreams though! At night, when the nightmares came, my screams would awaken Gene. Holding me in his strong arms, wiping away my tears as if I were a small child, he would reassure me that I was only dreaming. Once again I would fall asleep, only to have a recurrence of the whole thing within an hour or two.

Gene was patient and understanding with me. In the morning I would put on a plastic smile and act as if the night before had been a restful one. He called me his "sunshine girl," which helped me to feel a little better.

Most of our time was spent at his home because his mother lived with him. He hired a nurse to care for her through the day, but it was almost impossible to find anyone who would stay with her at night so that we could have a real date. Gene worried about my happiness with this arrangement and the stress of my helping to care for his mother.

I really didn't mind not going out. In fact it seemed like manna from heaven to be free of the fast pace that I had been living for so long.

It was only four months after we met that Gene asked me to marry him. There were so many things that I loved about him, it was easy to say yes. We decided to wait another four months so that we could plan a nice wedding and each take care of our business affairs, but I moved in with him right away.

My renter was not entirely surprised that I was going to marry Gene. He was pretty decent about being given such short notice to move.

By October of that year, my problems with the real estate commissioner had been resolved and the personal part of the money owed to the I.R.S. had been paid.

Education

Many times over the two and a half years since Brad's death I had wanted to simply run away, to be where no one knew anything about me. Just disappear, drop off the face of the earth. My choice not to run had nothing to do with being brave or standing my ground. It was because I knew there was no place to run. Memories and myself were what I wanted to escape, and that was impossible. No matter where I went or what I did, the memories of Brad would always be a part of me.

People often said "Time will take care of everything," and, "You will always feel the pain." By now I could see time alone was not a cure-all, and the pain of the memories was more than I had the energy to contend with. Was I stuck in my grief? It's not uncommon for people to become stuck in the paralyzing emptiness of grief, knowing it is impossible to move back in time and feeling that the pain will always be a strong part of one's life. It removes all hope for finding any peace.

By the time Gene and I were married on October 18, 1986, I was ready to give up.

When a boxer is being badly defeated, receiving too many damaging blows, a towel is thrown into the ring to indicate the fight is over, that he has given up. I felt that I was throwing in the towel. For two and a half years, most of the major decisions I made didn't seem to work out the way I felt they should. My general health was not good. If a cold or the flu were going around, I was sure to contract them. Anxiety about the future was now a way of life for me.

Gene showed me his love and was supportive of whatever I wanted to do. I wanted to do a lot of things, but was afraid to do anything, for fear of failure.

Gene encouraged me to talk about Brad's suicide and asked why I didn't speak of it in a more public manner. We had formed a motivational/training company that we named "Front Line Woman," and he felt that I should be able to work Brad's suicide into some of my speeches. He also kept asking all of those probing questions. Some of the answers I gave didn't feel right. There had to be more to this than what I knew.

Returning to the bookstore was fruitless, for there were still no books about suicide on the shelf, but I did find some about grief. These books helped me to start understanding the grieving process, but none of them offered any information about suicide.

I attended a grief recovery class at Loma Linda University Medical Center. This was a good class, but once again, no information on the grief of suicide.

It was here, however, I met another mother who had lost her son to suicide. This common bond was a magnet drawing us to each other. It was the first time either of us had met someone else with this experience. We felt set aside from the other people who were taking the class. We didn't necessarily feel our pain was any greater, just different. We had a sense of shame the other people didn't seem to have and our anger seemed more intense. We spoke in private about our feelings of wanting death for ourselves. The other people didn't speak of this, although they may have felt the same way. My own death wish was becoming less severe. As we talked, it dawned on me that death was not what we desired. What we wanted was to be with our children. Knowing they couldn't come to us, our desire was to go to them. We discussed the validity of my thoughts and agreed death was not, in fact, our wish, but rather a life without the emotional pain we were feeling.

It was after this experience that I made the decision to learn as much as I could about the causes of suicide and about the grief it brings. Like a detective looking for clues, I attended university classes through the psychology department. I took classes on self-esteem, awareness and change, confronting codependency, understanding children and adolescents of alcoholic families, etc.

The classes were interesting, and I learned a great many things from them, but I needed more. More information was becoming available on suicide prevention, so I read everything I could find on the subject. This led me to what few books there were, and these led me to the American Association of Suicidiology and the American Suicide Foundation.

At last I was learning the things I needed to help me better understand my son's death and my own pain.

Taboos and Stigmas

Stigmas and taboos cause us all a lot of unnecessary heartache. They start from a base of ignorance and fester like an ulcer in society. Left untreated, they bore deep beneath the surface, causing terrible pain, until they are cut away with education and understanding. The stigmas and taboos of suicide are the reason I felt such a sense of shame about the death of my son. I didn't understand this until I began to study the history of suicide.

Being a history buff, I already knew most ancient societies had no fear of suicide. In fact, they saw it as an acceptable way to die. In the Greek and Roman Empires, it was not uncommon for the government to supply a poison, hemlock, if one had a good reason and wished death by suicide.

What I didn't know was that in the early Christian era there was an epidemic of suicides. Life was difficult and many believers were eager to enter heaven. The church wanted to put a stop to it. So in the fourth century A.D., Saint Augustine persuaded the church to proclaim suicide a sin on the basis of its being self-murder. This pathetic attempt at suicide prevention didn't do much good.

In the 13th century A.D., Thomas Aquinas convinced the church to declare suicide a mortal sin with eternal damnation as the punishment. This helped a little, but was still not enough, so the church said a victim of suicide couldn't have religious rites or be buried in religious cemeteries.

Then laws were put into effect which offered harsh punishment to anyone who attempted suicide and to the families of the completed suicide. All property belonging to the victim was taken by the government. The body was violated, and often the head would be placed on a pole outside the city gate for all to see. Burial was often at a crossroad where the traffic would pass over the grave. The families were ridiculed with whispers of contempt, disgust, and scorn. They were the butt of cruel jokes. More often than not, they would have to move away from the town which had been their home. The stigma of suicide was disgrace, dishonor, humiliation, and shame. This setup a taboo against talking about suicide, and if one could not talk about it, one could not learn about it.

These attitudes didn't start to change until the 18th century. The laws were slowly changed. Even though there isn't any legal punishment in today's society, the stigmas and taboos are a punishment of their own. People have no idea how much pain they can inflict with some of their ignorant remarks.

One woman told me that my son would burn in hell for his action. Thank goodness most people are not so cruel, but often they didn't have to say it—I could see it in their face and eyes; I could hear it in their voice. This woman was devoutly religious and sincerely believed what she was saying.

Many churches and synagogues are working to help change these attitudes. The change is slow because the taboo is so deeply ingrained in us that even most professionals, like our religious leaders, teachers, nurses, doctors, and counselors, have not received the necessary education about suicide or the grieving process of the family.

When I first saw the statistics on suicide from The American Suicide Foundation and the National Institute of Mental Health, I found it hard to believe these rates could be so high. The reports state that suicide is the second major cause of death among high school and college students, the fourth major cause of death among adults ages 24–34, and that the highest adult suicide rates are found among men over the age of 50.

This information was alarming, but then I learned that these rates are based only on the reported deaths and that one-half to three times that many are covered up and never reported.

Many people take their own life in such a manner as to have the death appear to be an accident. An automobile is driven over a cliff or head-on into a tree, an accidental gunshot wound or a hanging that appears to have been an accident proves fatal, or someone steps in front of an oncoming train.

Sometimes the person who finds the body will remove evidence and make the death appear to have been an accident or homicide. Some people will go to all kinds of extremes in an attempt to have the word "suicide" removed from the death certificate. Stigmas and taboos are often the reasons for these cover-ups. How sad it is to face the death of someone we love and then find it necessary to fight the demons of ignorance.

After studying the history, I had a better understanding of my feelings and the attitudes of other people. The sting of ignorant remarks became less hurtful.

Thank goodness I had read the history books before attending a class at the University of California on self-esteem. The professor asked us the first day to introduce ourselves to someone we didn't know and tell them what kind of work we were involved in and any special interest we might have.

I turned to the woman sitting behind me and stated, "I'm the president of Front Line Woman, a company which conducts motivational/training programs, and my special interest is understanding suicide and the grief it causes." Instead of telling me her name, she informed me she had four children, one of which attempted suicide twice. She went on to say that she had taken the child to many doctors, yet she was still afraid and concerned the child would die.

There was not an opportunity to speak with her again until the last day of class, when the professor placed us in the same discussion group. We were instructed to tell the group about something we were either currently doing or had done in the past which was extremely difficult. This was easy for me, since I had just started writing a booklet about suicide. Everyone seemed to understand how difficult this task was and each was supportive in their own way.

Then we were asked to tell each other what it was we liked or respected about the other persons in our group. When it was this woman's turn (who had the suicidal child), she told me how wonderful she thought it was that I was writing about suicide and that she felt it should be helpful to many people. Then she said, "Most people write about their success; it's nice to see someone with the courage to write about their failures." Just as she made her statement, the professor announced, "Time's up."

With no chance to respond, I sat there as the poisoned arrows of her thoughtless words plunged deep into my heart. How I would have liked an opportunity to inform her that one has not failed in a relationship because their loved one died by suicide. I wonder if people who make statements like she did think that because their loved ones had not died by suicide, they are a success in their relationships.

The truth is none of us have been the perfect parent, spouse, sibling, or friend—we simply don't have that kind of power. We are human, and as humans, it is impossible for us to be perfect. We make mistakes in judgment.

At a point in time when I was deep in grief for my son, I did feel as if I had failed as a mother. Then I stopped to realize I have another son who has done outstandingly well in life and has a wonderful family of his own. I also realized that this child's success is because of the choices he has made in life and is not necessarily an indication of my skills as a parent.

Had the choice been mine, as to life or death for Brad, he would be alive today. No, death by suicide is not an indication of failure. It is, however, an indication of the extreme emotional pain with which that person was living.

This woman was speaking to me from her own fear of having failed her child. I feel so much empathy for people like her. We all have a tremendous amount to learn, not only about suicide, but about life in general.

Once I became aware of the death rate for suicide (35,000 to 40,000 each year and two to three times that many suspected to be suicide) and the fact that there are 500,000 reported suicide attempts each year—and still no one talking openly about it—I could see just how strong a hold the stigmas and taboos have on us all. I had a sense of sadness at seeing these numbers, and at the same time I felt better with the knowledge that I was far from alone in this matter.

Chapter Four

Eulogy

Gaining understanding about bereavement and suicide was helping me to feel better, but it wasn't enough. I still didn't feel at peace with myself. The hurtful dreams of Brad were not coming every night, but they still played their devilish tricks on me every other night or so.

It had now been four years since Brad's death, and I had accepted the idea that there would always be the tears when I spoke of him. I would always feel the pain like a knife being driven deep into my heart.

Although I was getting pretty good at relaxing my body and could recognize its signals of stress, I would have days of being so depressed I didn't want to leave the house. On those days I would set a time limit on the depression. It would come on slowly, so I didn't always recognize its suffocating grip right away. When the reality of what was happening became apparent, I would say to myself "Okay, Pat, if you insist on feeling miserable, do it all the way. You have two hours to wallow in it. Go to bed, pull the covers over your head, and cry or scream, do whatever you want. At the end of this time, however, you must get up, take a bath, put on pretty clothes, and go out into the world to be with other people."

Giving myself permission to be depressed and setting a time limit helped me to have a sense of control over my life. I didn't feel guilty about spending my time in this manner. Following my own instructions was difficult because depression is energy-robbing, and at times it required unbelievable effort just to get out of the bed, But with determination, I found it worked.

All memories of the past were painful, even the happy ones. Anxiety seemed to be a constant companion. I was starting to understand that when one spends too much time looking back, it brings depression, and when one looks too far ahead, it can bring on anxiety.

The importance of living life one day at a time was becoming more obvious. Although my progress was slow, I was grateful for the least bit of improvement. In the first year after Brad's death I couldn't even handle one day at a time. It was necessary for me, at times, to concentrate on life one second at a time just to make it through the day.

Very often while driving down the street a thought of Brad would cross my mind and I would burst into blinding tears, feeling as if my head and heart would explode from the pain. Sometimes I would scream and beat the steering wheel of the car, at other times I would bite my lip to keep from screaming.

Talking to myself seemed to help. I would say out loud something like, "Where am I right now? I'm driving in my car. Concentrate on what's going on. Look at the car just ahead, describe it in detail, read the license plate, what do the people look like who are in it, etc., etc." This silly game was difficult for me to play, but it forced my thoughts into the present.

Yes, I was grateful for any progress at all. To have even one night's sleep without dreams of Brad was another thing for which I was extremely grateful. Life without Brad was slowly becoming less gut-wrenching.

When I was asked to facilitate a grief recovery support group on a volunteer basis for the Women's Information and Resource Center, I felt unsure of myself. Had I reached a point where I could be of help to others? One thing was sure, I would understand how the people in grief were feeling. Loma Linda University Medical Center was offering a seminar on how to facilitate a grief recovery program, so I attended. Upon completion of the seminar, my confidence increased, and with Gene's continued encouragement I agreed to facilitate the group.

It was rewarding for me to be able to help the people who attended. My heart went out to each and every one of them. Some I remember especially. There was the daughter whose mother had died from kidney failure, the mother whose son was killed in a motorcycle accident, the lesbian whose mate of 15 years died of a heart attack. The more help and understanding I could bring to these people, the better I felt with my own grief.

One of the most rewarding experiences during this time was being able to help Carol, the friend who had sung so beautifully at Brad's funeral. Her sister had been killed in an automobile accident and she was having a difficult time with the grieving process. How unpredictable life is! For years I had felt a deep gratitude toward her and the kindness she had shown me but couldn't think of an appropriate way to express my feelings.

Writing thank-you notes at the time of Brad's death had been almost impossible. There were hundreds which needed to be written and mailed. The pain of this task was unbearable, so after writing about 50 of them, I told myself people would understand and gave up. I'm not sure if she received one, but even if she did, there aren't enough words to express the indebtedness I felt. Although I was extremely sorry for her loss, it was a wonderful feeling to at least be able to repay her kindness.

Good things came from this work, and the education I had been receiving in psychology was extremely helpful. Not one person who attended these meetings had lost a loved one to suicide. I wanted to shout from the rooftops what I had learned about suicide and the grief it brings but couldn't seem to come in contact with anyone who wanted to listen.

A minister I know called and asked me to give a presentation on the subject of suicide and grief. Wonderful! At last someone would listen! The program was well-advertised, and I knew the church had a membership of over 500. The minister said they usually had about 20 people attend the various programs which were held at the church each month.

My heart was pounding with excitement as I entered the church carrying the armload of handouts I had carefully selected from my resource material. Although it wasn't a surprise to me, it was a big disappointment when only one person showed up. The minister apologized profusely. Assuring him that I was not offended, I said, "At least you had the courage to try, and that is more than most people are willing to do."

March 26th fell on a Monday that year. It was a typical sunny, Southern California morning. Seated at the kitchen table with my first cup of coffee, I was not yet fully awake when the telephone's piercing ring startled me. We rarely receive calls at seven A.M., so it was with a sense of concern that I answered the phone. A female voice, so soft that I could barely determine what was being said, informed me that her name was Norma. Over the past year I had grown accustomed to hearing weak, listless voices like this one and it always meant the same thing—someone they loved had died!

"Pat, I don't know if you will remember me. I attended a self-improvement seminar you gave last year."

At first I didn't remember her, but as we talked my memory brought me a picture of this very attractive, petite woman in her mid-forties with dark hair and a pretty smile.

"Pat, I'm sorry to call this early, but I really need to talk to you. My son...well, my son, my son is..."

I could almost hear her tears falling as she spoke, and I could feel her pain. God, how I remembered that horrible pain! As I waited for her to continue speaking, my mind raced with thoughts of what kind of accident could have taken this son she loved so dearly. My own tears were flowing as she continued.

"My son is dead, and well, I would like to talk to you. I have a favor to ask of you. Can you meet with me today?"

"Of course I can," was my response. "May I ask how your son died?"

"It was on Friday. He...well, he shot himself."

Her voice was weak and faded out as she spoke. I wasn't sure that I had heard her right. I didn't ask her to repeat her painful words. We set our appointment for that afternoon. Thinking she had called me because of the grief support group, I suggested that we meet at the Women's Information Center. All morning I kept wondering if I had heard her right and what the favor was that she wanted. It really didn't matter, because I planned on agreeing to it, regardless of what she asked of me.

We arrived at the same time. I could see her shoulders drooped, heavy from grief, and her face was pain-stricken as she stepped from the car. Taking her in my arms, I was aware of how small she was. I held her longer, I'm sure, than she felt comfortable. My heart was filled with sadness and compassion. I so desperately wanted to take her pain away and felt helpless in the knowledge that no one could relieve her of this monumental heartache. At her suggestion, we sat outside on the patio under a grape arbor.

Her tear-filled eyes had an empty blank stare as she told the story of her son's death. With his new rifle and a bottle of liquor, he went to a motel where, some hours later, he shot himself. We talked for hours. At times her voice would be so weak I couldn't hear what she was saying. It didn't matter whether anyone heard her words or not;

she needed to talk. This excessive talking is normal behavior in the first stage of the grieving process.

As we talked, the flame of my own memories and pain were rekindled. When I shared the story of my son's death, she looked surprised.

"I remembered that your son had died a tragic death, but I didn't recall it being a suicide," she said. "Perhaps the favor I plan to ask of you will be too painful under the circumstances. I wanted you to deliver the eulogy at Kent's funeral. I know it's an unusual request to make of someone that didn't even know my son, but when I awoke at three o'clock this morning, for some reason, you came to mind, and I was remembering what an uplifting, optimistic way of speaking you have. I thought how nice it would be if you could deliver the eulogy. Then I called my friend, Sally. Do you remember her? She attended your seminar with me. When I told her what I was thinking and asked her opinion, she suggested that I act on my feelings and call you. If you feel that you don't want to do it, I'll understand."

My God! This couldn't be happening! What was she asking of me? I couldn't have heard her right!

"Are you telling me that you had no idea I facilitate a grief support group and you didn't know Brad died by suicide?" My face must have shown the disbelief and shock I felt.

"I'm sorry, Pat," she responded. "If you can't do it, I'll understand."

"No, no, of course I will. I'm just not sure how good a job I can do for you. It would be very emotional for me. This is such an important time in your life and I've never given a eulogy. Are you positive you want *me*?"

"I feel that in light of what you've told me about your son's death, you were meant to do this. Otherwise, why would I awake thinking of you?"

Although her voice was weak from grief, she showed the courage of a mother lion protecting its young as I heard her say, "Be open about the fact that Kent's death was a suicide. Tell the people some of the things you've told me about suicide. Help them to understand his emotional pain and the fact that I don't intend to be intimidated by the taboos and stigma."

Admiration was what I felt for her. Norma wasn't as fragile as her appearance deceivingly led one to believe, but she also didn't have an immunity to the pain which she was feeling. She had experienced all the hardships that being a single mother of three children can bring, having spent most of her adult life in that role.

We agreed that she would give me pictures of Kent and write out some of her thoughts about him so I could become acquainted with her child. She shared with me the details of his life as we spoke each day before the funeral.

Feeling extremely unsure of myself, I kept lamenting to Gene, "This is going to be so hard for me to do without losing my composure. It will feel like I'm delivering a eulogy for my own son. What if I make a mistake? I just hope I can bring some comfort to the family. This is so important. Do you think I should have said no? You know that I like to speak with humor; what if I say something stupid and unknowingly add to their pain? Who do I think I am anyway?" My dear husband would patiently listen to my self-doubt and then reassure me that he felt I was very qualified to handle the task.

In my mind, Brad and I discussed the matter. "Oh, Brad, what am I going to do? What if I start crying because of thinking about you?" The memory of his strong voice offering me encouragement the way he did when he was alive said, "Come on, Mom, you can do it. You're Super Mom! Remember when I was just a little boy lying in the hospital bed in a coma? The doctors told you I had died, but they had injected medication into my brain that brought me back to life. They told you if I had another brain seizure they wouldn't be able to bring me back a second time. You were to prepare yourself for my death. You said, "Who do you think you are, God? You didn't leave my bedside night or day. Come on Mom, you're stronger than you think you are. We've made it through tougher times than this. I'll be with you."

When I spoke with Norma about this self-doubt, she reassured me the family couldn't hurt any more than they already did and she still felt that I was meant to deliver the eulogy.

My confidence grew as I became acquainted with Kent through his mother. At 29, he was older than Brad but they were very much alike. Both were sensitive, kind, playful, cheerful, creative, and tried to please everyone. They found it hard to express emotion with words, had an extreme appreciation and love for children, high intelligence, and both were dyslexic. As more similarities became apparent, I started to feel as if I knew him extremely well.

For hours at a time I would stare at the screen of my word processor, hoping the right words would come to me, but the morning of the funeral arrived and I still had nothing written.

As I drove to the funeral, I thought of Brad and I prayed, "God, please help me to say the words that need to be said. Help me to bring comfort and understanding. Please let me be your servant."

When I arrived, there were already a few people waiting. It wasn't long before Norma arrived wearing an attractive black dress and very large sunglasses which she hoped would hide her swollen eyes. With a person on each side, holding her arms for support, she looked as if each step was leading her closer to the guillotine.

Tony is Norma's eldest son. He had car trouble on his way to the funeral, which caused a 45 minute delay. The 70 or so people present stood in small groups as they talked to pass the time. I went from group to group hoping that I looked relaxed and in control. Inside myself I was still praying and my palms were sweating. It's a good thing Tony arrived when he did, because the tension was about to get the best of me.

The plan was for me to speak, and then Norma's brother would read scripture from the Bible. He told me that he didn't feel this was the time or place to speak about suicide. Understanding that he was speaking from his own sadness and grief didn't help subside the anger his words had caused me to feel. My thoughts were of how typical his attitude was. Keep quiet; hide the shame; what will others think; nice people don't talk about such things in public. With a stern look and determined tone of voice, my response to him was: "I'm here at Norma's request. She asked me to speak on suicide and that's what I'm going to do. You can be assured that what I have to say will not be offensive to Kent or his family."

There were many people and a few small children among the ones who had come to honor Kent and his family that day. It would be difficult to hold their attention because everyone was restless after their long wait. The fire of my seething anger had squelched all self-doubts. As I stood between those people and Kent's cold lifeless body lying in its closed coffin, I felt it was my responsibility to protect not only his family and the memory of him from the vicious attacks of misunderstanding, but Brad as well.

In my introduction by the funeral director, the people were informed that my interest in suicide had come about after my own son's death by suicide. As I stepped forward to speak, I thought, "Here we go, Brad. God, please help us."

The words needed to paint a verbal picture of Kent came easily, for I had gotten to know and like this young man. My words reminded the people who had known him of how he went about showing his thoughtfulness by helping his friends to build patios, lay carpet, and many other laborious tasks. All he asked in return for his backbreaking labor was their friendship. It was a pleasure to speak of his sensitive nature and his apparent zest for life.

We laughed at some of the pranks he had pulled, cried for the loss of him, and felt concern for the negative side of his personality. Occasionally he would drink too much or use cocaine and become obnoxious and irresponsible. He had also shown signs of depression for some months before his death.

With sincere concern, I asked, "Why was he so depressed? Could it have been because he was fighting with his girlfriend, or did the depression cause the fighting? Could it have been because everything in his young life had seemed to be going wrong, or was everything going wrong because he was depressed? Could he have perhaps been physically ill for a long time with, for instance, diabetes, which left untreated can bring on true depression? Or maybe he was suffering from a lack of B vitamins, which play an important role in brain metabolism. A deficiency of vitamin C can also mimic depression. Left untreated, these deficiencies can cause one to become truly depressed. Was he perhaps a victim of any one or even all of these things?"

From the look on their faces, I could tell they were starting to see suicide in a little different light, so I kept going. They seemed surprised when I informed them that depression, leading to suicide, is the 10th leading cause of death in the United States, and that Hungary has the highest suicide rate in the world, with 48 percent of the deaths by suicide. I suggested they check with the National Institute of Mental Health to confirm my statement that at any one time there are approximately 16 million people in the United States who are suffering from depression. Not one person there knew that biological psychiatry is medical psychiatry which incorporates the latest scientific research in its approach to diagnosis, nor did they know that when a person has a major depression the chemicals in the brain change. Their understanding of these things was no more than mine had been before Brad's death, so I knew what I was about to say would be a total shock.

The brain is a very complicated mass of nerve cells and is essentially an electrical system. The nerves, something like wires, communicate their electrical signals to each other by way of a chemical messenger in the space, called the synapse, which runs between the nerve cells. One of the chemicals affected by depression is serontonin. A breakdown product of serotonin has been found to be a very good predictor of suicide. At this time, there is no convenient way to measure the breakdown. It can be measured in the spinal fluid by doing a spinal tap.

I told them that researchers are feverishly working on a way to identify certain chemicals in the blood to predict who is at risk of suicide. Of course, no one said it out loud, but they didn't have to, because I knew these looks of disbelief and was sure they were thinking the same things others had said, "A blood test that could predict suicide! You have to be kidding!"

"I overheard a number of you say, Kent just didn't seem the type. That's because there isn't a 'type' of person who dies by suicide. Depression is referred to as the 'common cold' of mental health. It plays no favorites. Age doesn't matter. It strikes very young children and the mature adult. It knows no social or economic boundary. Intellect and education can't stop it. This 'common cold' will strike most of us before we reach our teens and approximately 10 to 25 percent of us will suffer a major depression. It's sad to know that only one out of three will seek professional help and that this 'common cold' has a high likelihood of recurrence." With the information that there are 500,000 reported suicide attempts each year in the United States alone and that it's believed most attempts go unreported, I could see they were starting to understand that their families stood a greater chance of having a death by suicide than they had thought possible.

"Soon the shock of Kent's death will fade for all of you gathered here today, but the family will feel the pain for years to come. At some time in the future, you may feel inclined to wag your tongue and point a finger in the direction of this family, criticizing them, saying mean and hateful things behind their backs. If this happens, stop and look to yourself. Is your family perfect? Have you never said things to the people you love which you later wished you had left unsaid? Have you ever behaved in a less than perfect manner toward those people you love? Your honest answer has to be yes! Because there's no such thing as the perfect family! Some may be closer to perfection than others, but we are all human and as humans we make mistakes in judgment. What makes us think we have the right to be so critical of a family or feel that they are inferior to us, when the death has been a suicide!"

At this point, I told them the history of suicide and explained this is why the family may feel a sense of shame. I asked them, or maybe I should say begged them, to stop using the word "committed" when speaking of a suicide to the family. As an example, I said, Brad's death was the result "of" a gunshot wound and "by" suicide. "Committed" sounds so cold and impersonal. Most of the people were leaning forward in their seats, listening intently to what was being said.

Turning to face Kent's coffin, I said, "Kent, your mother, Norma, and I solemnly promise you, from this day forward we will do everything within our power to not only educate ourselves in regard to suicide, but to speak out against the taboos and stigmas at every opportunity—to bring understanding of the emotional pain of depression which often precedes a death by suicide, and to protect the memory of you. Believe me Kent! It's a sincere promise!

Norma's brother was the first of many to say, "I'm so very glad you were here today. What you said has helped me feel much better. You were right, those things did need to be said. Thank you!"

For me to make it through that day without tears was a small miracle. The anger and determination I had felt helped to build the dam which held back my tears. Although I was emotionally and physically exhausted afterwards, I felt better for having had the opportunity to speak out, to fight back. The feeling that my words had brought a small degree of comfort to the family was wonderful.

Caring People

It's interesting to see how many people show their support in a time of crisis. They rally around the family with a morbid curiosity, making pledges of long-term assistance which will rarely ever be kept. These people mean well and their actions are deeply appreciated by the person or person in need. But as time wears on, the commitment to their pledges becomes less important to them. The urgency of their own lives takes precedence, which is understandable.

There really isn't much anyone can do to help us through our grieving process. The journey to recovery is, for the most part, a solitary experience. One thing that can be done is to listen! Just listen and not try to make sense of what is being said. To sit quietly and let the griever tell the story of how the death occurred as many times as they feel the need. To have someone listen to the repeated descriptions of the deceased person's life is of true help.

Often people will make the mistake of saying, "I know how you feel." This is insulting and hurtful. Unless they have had a loved one die by suicide, there is no way they can even come close to "knowing" how you feel. Even those of us who have had this experience don't "know" how the other person feels, but we can understand the emotional pain of the experience. When someone who has not lived through this pain says, "I know how you feel," or "I understand how you feel," it sounds as if they are attempting to minimize our pain.

Another hurtful thing which is said all too often is: "You're so strong to live with the pain. I don't know how you do it! I couldn't!" The first few times this was said to me, my response was, "I'm not sure I can." The truth was, I didn't want to go on living with this unbearable pain and I certainly didn't feel "strong" enough to live with it. After repeatedly hearing different people make comments about how "strong" I was, a feeling of guilt would come over me. If no one else could live with this and I was doing it, then something must be wrong with me! On the one hand, I knew this wasn't true, but on the other, I was ready to feel guilty about anything. Not having anyone to speak with who had lost a loved one to suicide, I didn't know that these feelings are normal. At least Norma would have the benefit of my experience!

Norma had a number of friends who kept their pledge of assistance. The one who did the most to help her was Sally. Although Sally was in a new marriage, she asked Normal to be her house guest and took care of her for a few weeks. Speaking with each of them almost every day, I was amazed at the degree of sensitivity and understanding Sally showed. When I asked her about this, she shared the fact that she had made an attempt at suicide a few years earlier, so she understood the state of mind Kent must have been in at the time of his death. When her attempt was made, she had been extremely depressed for some months. Feeling hopeless and as if she were a burden to her family, each day she sank deeper and deeper into the pits of depression. She described it as a deep, black, bottomless hole that once you enter, you can't find a way out of. She said that she felt as if she was giving her family a gift with her death. They wouldn't have to be bothered with her or her troubles any longer. Life was so unbearably miserable for her, and the feeling that it would never be any better was overpowering.

After this attempt at death, she entered long-term psychotherapy and was now better able to cope with the stress of life as it came her way. Although Sally is determined to live a happy life, her greatest fear is that the extreme depression will someday return and she will slip once again into that "deep, black, bottomless hole."

It was with certainty that I could relate to her feelings. After one of our many conversations about depression, I wrote in my journal:

DEPRESSION

Oh, how I envy the people who have never traveled to the pits of hell, wearing a shroud of hopelessness. Astride the wild black steed of depression, with his blazing red eyes, as he takes you on that maddening ride of a downward spiral into the bowels of hell.

Those who haven't taken this journey can't possibly understand the pain or hopelessness of it. Although many never travel all the way to the pits of hell, few people escape the trip entirely.

The return trip is a slow and difficult one. It's much like attempting to climb an embankment with many moss-covered stones protruding from it. The climber must be very careful to avoid the innocent-looking moss, for once touched, they stand the chance of slipping back into that
"deep, black, bottomless hole."

Watching Norma struggle through that first heartbreaking year of mourning was difficult. We spent long hours talking on the telephone and over lunch. Right from the beginning, I suggested that she seek professional counseling. Reassuring her that she could survive this pain was my primary objective. When Norma returned from her first visit with the doctor, she had a prescription for an antidepressant. Taking the medication helped her the first few weeks. A side effect to it was that she slept until very late in the day. As long as she was not working, this wasn't a problem, but after returning to work she couldn't contend with the feeling of being drugged. Although the doctor attempted to resolve the problem, nothing seemed to help. Soon she lost confidence in not only the medication but the doctor as well.

One day, about five months after Kent's death, I received a call from Sally. "Pat, I'm really concerned about Norma. I feel she is suicidal. Will you talk to her?"

I hadn't spoken with Norma for about three weeks. Although she had appeared to be doing well, I wasn't surprised to hear she felt suicidal. The surprise was in the fact that she had not felt this way sooner.

When I spoke with her to make sure she would be home, I didn't mention the call from Sally. Arriving at her home, I found her in a state of depression. She couldn't see any point to continuing the struggle of life. Feeling hopeless and alone, she wanted to end her life.

As we talked, I asked, "If you had the choice of putting an end to your life or an end to your problems and pain, which would you choose."

"Well, of course I'd choose an end to the problems and pain," was her response.

"Then you don't really want to die! Maybe what you desire are solutions to your difficulties."

She sat quietly as I continued to speak. "Nothing will ever bring our children back. We don't get a chance to do it over again. No matter how many times we say, 'I should have done this or that differently,' it won't change a thing. The decisions we've made as mothers haven't always been the best, but they haven't always been the worst either.

"If our love could have kept them alive, they would be with us today. They couldn't see any solutions to their problems and pain. As adults, we can't always see solutions when we are in emotional pain. We can't give our children or anyone else what we don't have. We can't show them the way if we can't see it ourselves. This is not their fault or our fault; it's just a fact of life.

"We don't have the power to go back and 'fix' the past. It will always remain as it is. We don't have a crystal ball that will tell us what the future holds, and if we did, it would take the excitement and adventure out of life. All we can be sure of is this moment in time. Our control is in the now. This second, right now, is all we can be sure of having. What we do with it is up to us.

"The only person that you are guaranteed to spend your entire life with is yourself. This is a truth for each of us and yet most of us treat ourselves far worse than we do anyone else we know. We wrongfully condemn ourselves many times throughout the day, day after day, week after week, and year after year. If we treated other people this way, no one would choose to be around us. Try giving yourself the same consideration you would extend to others. Please believe me when I say this horrible pain of Kent's death will pass. It takes a long time, but someday it will stop."

We talked about how unnatural it seems for a child to precede a parent in death. Norma said, "I never gave a thought to one of my children dying before me."

This was an issue I had to face years before Brad's death. Steve's choice of a military career and Brad's clinical death had left me very aware that death doesn't always take a chronological number.

The next hour was spent on finding solutions to her immediate needs. How to increase her income was at the top of our list. Soon she showed sings of feeling more in control of her life. I felt sure that she would be all right for now.

As I left, my parting words were to encourage her to attend the Hope After Suicide support group which I had founded a few weeks after Kent's death. "You could benefit from the support of these people in the group. They will understand what you are going through and they truly care about what happens to each other. Please join us!"

Norma had only attended one of these meetings. No matter how I encouraged her to return, she just couldn't seem to do it. Talking about the death of a loved one can be extremely painful, but it is the very thing that will speed the healing process.

In the beginning, it is difficult for anyone to sit with a group of strangers and say the relationship and name of the deceased, the manner of death, and the date it occurred. The first few times I did this, there was a lump in my throat the size of a tennis ball.

"My...son...Brad...shot...himself...to...death...on...February...19th...1984." How it hurt to say those words, but it's the saying of it, over and over, in front of other people, that helps one to accept the death as a reality.

A Common Bond

While I was planning the eulogy for Kent, I had felt a need to check some of my information about suicide, so I called the local Crisis Assessment Team. The man who answered was Robert Lefler, L.C.S.W. Since he was willing to be of help, we set a time for me to stop by his office at the hospital. The congested environment in which we live is not conducive to offers of help to strangers, so I was a little surprised that this busy man would be willing to meet with me.

Extending his large hand, this extremely tall, ruggedly good-looking man, with an infectious smile, said, "Hi! I'm Bob." As we talked about the grief of suicide, I told him how difficult it had been for me to meet anyone with whom I could speak, who had lost someone they loved to suicide. His response was, "I'm sure there are many other people who feel as you do. Why don't you start a support group?"

"Where would I hold the meetings?" I asked.

"Are you asking me if the hospital will make a meeting room available for this use?"

"Well, yes, I guess I am."

Working with suicide, as he does, he truly understood the community's need for this type of support group. Within a few days, he called to say I had a place to hold the meetings. When he suggested that he attend the first meeting in order to observe my abilities, I was very grateful for his assistance. I was also impressed with the fact that he was willing to give up his free time to help people in need. This compassionate man has been a strong right arm to my efforts. He's the one I call on when I need a better understanding of a particular situation or to locate help for the people in the group. The kindness and understanding he shows everyone makes him an unsung hero, in my eyes.

The support group has been a wonderful avenue for me to observe many of the things which I'd read about but hadn't necessarily experienced. Although we share many of the same feelings and heartaches, each loss has something different about it. The widow may feel her deceased husband in bed with her at night. Young widows have the very real fear that their children will become suicidal. I wasn't married at the time of Brad's death, so I hadn't experienced the tremendous strain that the death of a child can place on a marriage.

Brothers and sisters of a suicide victim seem to feel a great deal of anger and frustration. They have been thrown into the temporary role as caretaker for the parents, and often don't know what to do or what is expected from them. Friends of the suicide victim have a difficult time because they aren't really a part of the family unit and often feel unsure of where they now fit in. Will their presence serve as a hurtful reminder, or will they be welcomed by the family?

Some people attempt or threaten suicide many times before they die. Each time this happens, the family, needless to say, is an emotional wreck. This behavior may go on for years before the death occurs. The family members become worn down emotionally and often have an understandable sense of relief when the death occurs. They don't want their loved ones to die, but there is a feeling of relief. No more calling 911, and no more panic when the phone rings, if they don't know where he/she is! Certainly anyone who has lived with this kind of worry and tension has a right to feel relief when it is over. Feeling the relief doesn't mean the love is any less or that the grief will be any easier.

It's fascinating to see how this common bond of a death by suicide pulls us together. The rich, the poor, those who are well-educated and people with minimal education, the young, and the old, all offering support to one another. Each understanding the other's pain. After attending these meetings, one quickly learns suicide has no boundaries.

The two questions most frequently asked are: "Why?" and "Will the pain ever stop?" I can't answer the "Why?" Each person will have to be their own detective to find the cause of the depression that brought on the suicidal behavior. In the beginning of the search for "Why?" most people attempt to place blame. We lash out in our pain, making accusations of fault not only toward others but to ourselves. Even if we find one person, one group of people, or one circumstance to place the blame on, it won't bring back the one we love. In fact it will only torment and frustrate, causing bitterness. The bitterness can become like a cancer; it devours the person in whom it lives. These feelings will restrict the healing process and bring nothing but more pain.

It's my opinion that no one thing brings about a suicide. Instead it's the compounding of many real or imagined, small and large hurts, disappointments, embarrassments, and a sense of failure, over the years. None of us really knows how much emotional pain the other is living with. We don't hear the silent tears falling on their pillows. We don't hear the silent screams for help until it's too late.

Keep asking yourself "Why?" until you find your own answers. No one else can bring you satisfaction.

When I'm asked, "Will the pain ever stop?" my honest answer is: "Yes, the raw pain can be stopped if you work at making it happen, but time alone will not completely stop it."

Feeling the pain is not only natural, it's necessary. You don't cure grief, you heal through it. If grief is viewed as something to be avoided, it can bring only more pain. Trying to go on as if nothing has changed is impossible.

Unrecognized, unhealed grief leaves festering wounds and can be a factor in a surprising amount of stress-related diseases. Each of us has to work through the pain of grief in our own way. How long it takes depends on the individual. Some people, like myself, have many issues to resolve; others only have a few. Suicide attacks one's self-esteem. If your self-esteem is low to begin with, as mine was, then you are in for a difficult time and it will take longer to work through the pain. However long it takes for your personal grieving process is okay. Don't let anyone rush you. It's over when it's over.

There are ways you can help yourself to have a more complete recovery and inner peace. Seeking professional counseling, of course, is the most obvious path to take and is what I suggest to the people in my support group. The one thing that will be of the most help is talking about the death, and a support group is the best place to do your talking. To know that you are not alone in this experience is extremely important. Educating yourself about suicide is another important part of healing, and understanding helps bring about acceptance.

Learning to take care of yourself is vital to recovery. Understand that all relationships will end on a note of sadness, because one of the two people will change their mind about how they feel, or one of the two will die. This means you are the only person that you are guaranteed to spend 100 percent of your life with. This is why we cherish our relationships with others, yet we know in our heart that they are temporary.

For some people it's easy to love and care for others, but they don't feel it's right to love and care for themselves. Give yourself permission to be your own caretaker, and be good to yourself. Don't be afraid to cry. Tears are liquid emotion and help you to heal. Be patient with yourself. Take the time to learn relaxation techniques and then use them every day.

Writing down what you are thinking and feeling can be of tremendous help. Be willing to see humor, laugh with others and at yourself. This relieves the stress and is healing. Reach out to help others.

These are some of the things you can do to help make the pain become less intense and you will discover more things yourself.

The knife that has been driven deep into your heart will be slowly removed. The sharp pain you now feel will fade, but you will always be aware of the scar.

My own evidence of this was on my third visit to the mausoleum, which was six years after Brad's death. The first two visits were horribly painful. I was racked with tears of guilt and longing. This time was different. I had a lump in my throat and a sad feeling, but the feeling of guilt had changed into regret. I knew my grieving was complete. Brad will always be loved and live in my heart. The memory of him will never fade. I'll always be sad when I think of his death, but the horrible pain is gone.

Chapter Five

Alcohol and Drugs

As I went about my studies, piecing together the puzzle of my past, the influence alcohol had on every facet of our family life became more apparent. This poison had brought an end to 18 years of marriage. Its mind-controlling effect had caused us all embarrassment, shame, humiliation, and pain. Someone unfamiliar with how alcohol controls a family may have a misconception that the drinker is a nonproductive bum. This is far from true. Often the drinker has an ability to advance in their job or business, getting promotions and awards for distinction. Satisfactory job performance can remain intact until very late in the illness. This was certainly true in my family.

The web of alcoholism is most often woven slowly and methodically, entrapping those who stay near. Slowly the drinking is increased. A little too much wine with dinner, mixed drinks become a little stronger each time a drink is made by the drinker, or a few more beers after a round of golf.

Soon the family finds itself caught in the web and the more they struggle against it, the tighter its hold becomes, until they feel as if the air of life has been choked from them.

Verbal abuse from the drinker becomes an accepted way of life. Oh, the words hurt and are fought against, but they are accepted as truth. Never knowing what to expect in the way of attitude or behavior from the drinker causes extreme stress for the family. Sometimes the drinker will be extremely happy, playful, loud, and boastful, at other times quiet, brooding, and pensive, and at another time the behavior will be angry and abusive. All of these behaviors can show up within seconds of one another, so the family is always on guard, trying to say and do the right thing to keep the drinker happy. Peace at any price!

The drinker has an unspoken control. Soon the family learns to mistrust their own judgment and ability to cope with life. It's at this point that some drinkers play the game called "Drink With Me Or I'll Find Someone Who Will." Once the co-dependent is convinced that they can't function without the relationship, they often tend to go along with much of what the drinker wants from them. Drinking then becomes the center of activity, not only socially, but in the home. In my marriage, it took 12 years to reach this point.

It was around the time I began drinking with him that we started moving up the ladder of success at a rapid pace. Outsiders would often look at our little family with envy, saying such things as: "How do you do it? Your children are so well-mannered. Steve has outstanding achievements. Brad overcame that horrible accident. They've never been in any kind of trouble. You have a good marriage. It's obvious how much you all love each other, and on top of all that you're financially successful." These people would solicit our advice about overcoming the hardships of life, rearing children, and financial matters. Yes, we were admired and respected by everyone who didn't come too close. Our divorce came as a shock to those people.

By staying in this relationship for so many years, I felt that I was holding the family together, doing what was best for the children and myself. A consistent command to the children was, "go to your room," as if they could be spared the hurt of our arguing by this action. The constant tension with which we lived was very painful. My years of living with attacks of severe nervous indigestion should have served as a warning for me to get out of that relationship. I've never had another attack like that since my divorce. It was only after being divorced that I could start to see clearly the damaging effects of alcohol and our dysfunctional family life.

The truth of this made me feel sick to my stomach the day I read a pamphlet on teen suicide from the American Psychiatric Association, which states, in part: Adolescents who consider suicide generally feel alone, hopeless, and rejected. They are more vulnerable to having these feelings if they have been abused, feel they have been humiliated recently in front of family or friends, have parents with alcohol or drug problems, or have a family life with parental discord, disruptions, separation, or divorce. It also states that a teenager may be depressed and/or suicidal without any of these problems. As I read this pamphlet, my heart felt as if it would break from pain and tears fell from my eyes like drops of acid burning deep into my very soul. I could see Brad's young sad face the way it looked when he cried.

Looking at my past is painful and no matter how many times I ask myself, "What if I had done this or that," it will not change one thing. The choices I made before and after Brad's death were not always the best, but they were what I believed to be best at the time. So I must learn to accept my past as just that, "*past*," and move forward with my life.

Alcohol and/or illegal drugs have destroyed many lives and families. People who abuse alcohol and drugs cause as much or more damage to the people they profess to love as they do to themselves. In today's society we often hear an alcoholic drink referred to as "a little pick-me-up," and a little lift is just what you get. When the high starts to wear off, depression sets in. If you don't consume alcohol or use drugs very often, you may not notice this slightly depressed state of mind. The more often one uses these chemicals, the greater the depression will become. Most alcohol and drug abusers, especially of cocaine, have a terrible time with depression. Anyone who has done biological research can tell you this is because the chemicals in these drugs end up substituting for the natural brain chemicals.

According to The Fifth Special Report to the Congress on Alcohol and Health (1983), as many as 80 percent of people who attempt suicide have been drinking at the time. Alcohol is a depressant. This may have been the first time some of these people ever had a drink of alcohol. They may have taken it for the false courage it brings.

When a young person dies by suicide, one of the first things many people ask is, "Was he/she on drugs?" It is interesting to know that most young people who take their own life are *not* users of illegal drugs. Some parents feel that it would be easier to answer questions about the death if their child had been on drugs. They seem to feel that if the child were a user of illegal drugs, it would satisfy their most difficult questions: "Why?"

Lessons

Brad's death has taught me many things. This experience has brought me to a level of honesty with myself and others I would never have dreamed possible. It has forced me to examine every facet of myself, my beliefs, my values, and my judgment. I've had to discard what was not working and build on what was. Yes, I've had to take a good look at myself. There were many things I didn't like, but more that I did. His death has taught me I don't have any control over other people's behavior, only my own. I've learned that what the people I love do is not a reflection of who I am.

One of the hardest lessons has been not to worry about the things which I can't control.

Like:

- My son, Steve, had two more surgeries on his knees and received a medical discharge from the army. This was extremely difficult for him and I wanted to help, but there wasn't anything I could do.
- We had known for years my mother has polycystic multiple organ disease of her kidneys and liver. Now she has been told she has a chemical imbalance. She suffers with depression, anxiety, and panic attacks. I would like to make these things better for her, but I don't have the power.
- My sister Carol inherited this disease from our mother. All of her internal organs are affected by polycystic multiple organ disease. It makes me sad to watch her body swell from the cysts, but there isn't any way I can take the pain away from her.

I can offer encouragement, emotional support, do small helpful things, and show my love for them, but beyond that, I have no control. Brad's death has made me aware of how precious life is and just how quickly it can be taken away. Knowing this, it's hard at times not to get carried away with worry for my family, but one of the most important things I've learned is the influence my thoughts have over my life. So when I start to worry, I take control of my thoughts, get them into the present, and then I'm okay.

I've learned to accept my vulnerability. I no longer feel that I have to be strong all of the time—it's okay to show my true feelings.

My son's suicide brought me hell on earth; my own death was more desirable than a lifetime of anguish. Then a determination to survive came about. Once mere survival was assured, I wanted more, to be whole and happy. I wasn't sure this could be done without Brad. As I started paying attention to the abundance of important lessons to be learned, both large and small, I realized my life would be whatever I make it.

I wasn't given a choice as to his living or dying, but I do have a choice as to how I handle the fact that he is dead.

I've seen people who have stayed in the misery of grief for a lifetime. I knew I didn't want to live my life in a continued state of pain. In the beginning, grief is in control, but it doesn't have to stay that way.

Brad will always be a part of me and I'll continue to miss him, but grieving year after year isn't proof of my love for him. This kind of holding on is only proof of unresolved issues, not of love. I think of him each and every day, but the pain is gone. It hurt Brad to see me be sad. He liked me best when I was happy and smiling. He felt pride in me when I showed courage in the face of adversity. It's important that I live my life with pride, dignity, fulfillment, and happiness. Not only because it honors the memory of him, but because I have an obligation to myself and the rest of my family to be the very best I'm capable of being. It's through the pain of Brad's death that I've learned to do this, one day at a time.

My happiness isn't contingent on other people, rather on how I react to those people and the things they do.

Learning to forgive myself and reaching out to help others do the same has helped me to find inner peace.

The Forgotten

Suicide has a profound effect on everyone close to it. One group of people who rarely receive much compassion or understanding when a suicide occurs are the health-care professionals. An attitude of "they should have known—they should have seen it coming" prevails, not only among the family, but the professionals as well. Most of these people chose their careers because of a sincere desire to help others lead a healthier and happier life. They spend a great deal of money and years being educated in their efforts. When someone under their care dies by suicide, they temporarily question their own ability to be of help. Often they have spent months helping a person who is hiding their suicidal thoughts, so the suicide comes as a surprise.

One Friday afternoon I received a call from the mental health department of a local hospital. The person placing the call was obviously under stress. An outpatient died by suicide. She had been extremely popular with the other patients and the staff. A gregarious person, she was referred to as the "cheerleader" of her group therapy. Bubbly and playful, she always had a word of encouragement for everyone. Her suicide came as a complete shock to the staff. On Monday, they would have to inform the group of her death, and their own feeling of shock had left them unsure of the best way to go about it. It was agreed I would attend the therapy session and talk to the group about suicide and grief.

My heart went out to the staff. Their eyes were red from the tears and lack of sleep. They had such sincere concern for each person. Staff, doctor, patients, and I talked for about three hours that day, each person sharing their pain and confusion. Those patients are fortunate to have such an openly loving and compassionate staff—far too many are not that fortunate.

It's easy for us to find fault with the professionals, especially when the care given may have been less than satisfactory. Most of the time the professional is doing their best and sincerely wants the patient to recover. Sometimes we feel these people have an immunity to the pain of a suicide. They are educated to understand emotions, not to be free of them. Shock, emotional pain, and a temporary feeling of failure are all part of their experience with suicide, just as with the rest of us. Their knowledge helps them to deal with these feelings, but be assured most do feel them to some extent.

Taking Care of Yourself

The stress of mourning can cause you to feel fatigued and emotionally strung out. Unless you take care of yourself, the tension and sleepless nights will leave you unable to make good decisions regarding the complex problems you will have to face. Staying mentally and physically healthy when you are under so much stress is extremely important.

There are many simple things you can do to help yourself. The most important truth to understand is: *You are stronger than you think you are. You will survive this tragedy.*

Simple Relaxation

When we are tense, the muscles that seem to tighten immediately are those in the back of the neck, through the shoulders and the shoulder blades, and into the lower back. You may also feel tightening muscles in the jaw and/or in the legs. There may be a sense that your heart is "pounding," that your pulse rate has become rapid.

Tension is the opposite of relaxation. The body consumes more energy when it's tense. During relaxation, the body restores energy. Relaxation will increase your coping power. You can't *make* yourself relax. You have to let it happen. It's important to be in a quiet room or a place where you will not be interrupted.

There are many techniques to help reduce muscle tension and decrease anxiety. The sequence below is the one I've had the most success with.

◆◆◆

Sit in a comfortable chair or lie on a couch or bed. Loosen or remove any tight clothing. Remove your shoes, but make sure your feet are warm. Make sure your neck is comfortable. You may want a pillow under your knees to help the lower back muscles relax. You should not cross your arms or legs.

◆◆◆

Close your eyes. Inhale slowly and deeply through your nose. Breathe so that your stomach pushes out. As you breathe in, count slowly to six, and as you breathe out, through your mouth, count slowly to eight.

Repeat this exercise four or five times, then breathe normally and rest quietly for two or three minutes.

◆◆◆

Now, take a deep breath and hold it. Stretch your toes, pulling them up toward your head. Feel the tension in your feet, calf, and leg muscles. Now let the tension flow out as you breathe out, slowly.

Repeat this three times.

◆◆◆

Take a deep breath. Make a fist of each hand and tighten the shoulder and neck muscles as much as you can. Feel the tension build. Now breathe out and let it all go; feel it flow out of your body.

Repeat this three times.

◆◆◆

Take a deep breath. Scrunch up your face and bite down as hard as you can. Feel the tension. Now breathe out and let it go.

Repeat this three times.

◆◆◆

Take a deep breath. Tense the muscles in your stomach, abdomen, anus, and genitals as hard as you can. Hold that tension.

Now breathe out and let it go.

Repeat this three times.

◆◆◆

Take a deep breath. Tighten all the muscles in your entire body. Hold the tension as long as you can, then breathe out and let the tension go. Feel all the tension flow out of your body.

Repeat this three times.

Deep Relaxation

Deep relaxation involves a mental discipline which becomes the key to deep inner serenity. Think about the following sentences, one by one. When you have experienced in your body the thought contained in your mind, move to the next sentence. This is a step-by-step process by which you can achieve deep relaxation and develop mental discipline.

◆◆◆

With your eyes closed, repeat each sentence slowly to yourself, then try to experience what it says.

"I am feeling relaxed now. My mind is quiet. I feel at peace. My forehead and scalp are completely relaxed; all the muscles are at rest. All the muscles in my face are relaxed and limp. My jaw drops open just a little so my teeth no longer touch. I let go and relax. My neck muscles are completely relaxed and tranquil; all the tension is gone. The muscles in my shoulders are relaxed. This feeling of relaxation is moving down my arms to the elbows, down the forearms to my hands and my fingers. My arms feel limp and dangle from the frame of my body. As I take a deep breath and relax, all of the tightness and tenseness is leaving my body. My breathing is now normal and relaxed as I relax my stomach muscles. I feel the relaxation moving down both sides of my spine; into my waist, buttocks, and thighs, down to my knees. The relaxation is moving into the calves of my legs, my ankles, my feet, even my toes are relaxed. Now my entire body is heavy with relaxation. I can feel the gravity of the earth pulling me back against the [bed] and my body is getting heavier and heavier with relaxation. I'm completely relaxed from the top of my head to the tips of my toes."

◆◆◆

Now, in your mind, go to the most peaceful place you can remember seeing or being in. This place may be the beach at sunset, with the waves of the ocean pounding on the shore, or the mountains with the sound of the wind blowing through tall pine trees. It could be where you played as a child. See yourself alone in this special, private place.

Wherever it is, recall it in every detail and feel the peace that it brings.

As you enjoy being in this serene place, say these things to yourself:

"I am letting go of any feelings of anger or resentment that I may have. I will rise above these harmful feelings, because I understand they are of more harm to me than to anyone else."

Picture in your mind these, or any other negative feelings, moving away from you. Notice them getting smaller as they move away, until you can no longer see them.

Now slowly return to your present reality. Continue to rest comfortably. Let your mind focus on the pleasant feeling and all that is good.

◆◆◆

It took me many months to learn to do the last part of this exercise. When I first started instructing myself to let go of the anger and resentment, it felt like a lie and was very uncomfortable.

This exercise really goes beyond relaxation and into inner healing. It has been a tremendous help to me and to other people I've worked with.

Sleep

At the best of times, it can be difficult to get a good night's rest, but when you are mourning the death of a loved one, it can seem impossible. Without the proper rest, we get up feeling tired and irritable. This can cause difficulty in coping with our emotions.

When the body is tired and we still can't sleep, it's because our minds are working overtime. They replay old conservations and bring up worries about the future. Things always seem worse at night, when we feel powerless to do anything about them. Fortunately there are ways of slowing the mind down so that we can get our much needed rest.

The first thing to do is avoid all stimulants for at least six hours prior to bedtime. This includes no reading of the newspaper or watching the news on television, no coffee, tea, or hot chocolate, and no sugar.

Second, do some kind of *mild* exercise about one hour before bedtime. If possible, go for a short walk or try running in place.

Third, write out the things you are thinking about. Make a list of the things you plan to do the next day. Write about anything that is on your mind.

Fourth, drink warm milk or take two calcium tablets. Calcium soothes the nerves. Then take a warm—not hot—bath.

Fifth, do the deep-breathing and/or the deep relaxation exercise, and tell yourself that you will have a good night's rest.

If you still can't go to sleep or have gone to sleep and then awake in the night, don't stay in bed. Get up—and don't go back to bed until you feel tired. Write about the things you are thinking and feeling. Your writing doesn't have to make sense or be written in a proper way. This is just a way to dump the thoughts that are keeping you from sleeping.

There are some very good environment audiotapes available with such sounds as: the ocean, a thunderstorm, a country stream, the wind in the trees, a gentle rain in the forest, and many other pleasant, restful sounds. I've found these tapes to be relaxing and helpful when played at night as I drift off to sleep. They can be found at most record stores.

Exercise

Mourning uses an immense amount of energy—we feel exhausted most of the time. There are days when it takes a great deal of effort just to get out of bed. Every muscle in your body seems to ache. The simple process of putting one foot in front of the other to walk up two or three steps can feel like you are climbing Mount Everest.

It may sound crazy, but this is the very time you need to get out of the house. Go for a walk, swim, ride a bike, or play tennis. If you can't think of anything to do, you may want to work in your yard or clean your house or garage. Do anything that is physical exercise.

Physical exercise helps to fight depression, and depression is a very large part of mourning. A short walk of 20 minutes or so each day will do wonders for the way you feel.

Nutrition

Another element to remember is nutrition. Some people tend to stop eating when they are depressed; others—like me—eat everything in sight. Neither way is good.

Make sure your diet consists of healthy foods: fresh fruit and vegetables, lean meat products, whole-grain breads and cereals, and milk or yogurt. Ask your doctor for nutritional guidelines.

While you're talking to your doctor about nutrition, ask about vitamin supplements. Some doctors feel they are helpful and others say they are a waste of money. I believe we need all the help we can get to feel better when we are in mourning.

I recommend to the people who attend my "Hope After Suicide" program that they "eat for nutrition" and take an "herbal diuretic, vitamins C, B-6, and/or B-complex, calcium-magnesium, and valerian." Of course, you should always ask your doctor's opinion before undertaking such a program. The people who stay with this program for as little as a week report that they do seem to feel better.

Another thing I recommend is to avoid sugar, alcohol, caffeine, chocolate, and white flour. All of these can cause nervousness, headaches, elevated blood pressure, confusion, and insomnia.

Remember these important facts:

- You may want to withdraw from it all, but you are not "going crazy."
- Give yourself permission to cry as much as you feel you need to. This is an important part of the mourning. You may find yourself crying for no obvious reason. This spontaneous crying will become less frequent with time.
- Your most important job at this time is to take care of yourself. Physically, emotionally, and spiritually.

I Believe in Me

Suicide is a thief that steals more than the life of people we love—it also robs us of our belief in ourselves. It takes away our self-esteem and our self-confidence. Though we can never get back the person it took from us, we can rebuild our belief in ourselves.

Reading these statements every day until they become part of your thinking will help you to start rebuilding your belief in yourself.

1. I am in charge of my own life.
2. My number one responsibility is my own growth and well-being.
3. The better I am to myself, the better I will be to others.

4. I refuse to be put down by the attitudes or opinions of others.
5. I do not need to prove myself to anyone. I need only to express myself as honestly and as effectively as I am capable.
6. My emotional well-being is dependent primarily on how I love myself.
7. I am kind and gentle towards myself.
8. Every experience I have in life (even the unpleasant ones) contributes to my learning and growth.
9. I am a unique and precious human being, always doing the best I can, always growing in wisdom and love.
10. I live life one day at a time.

Spirituality

The four aspects of our being are: physical, emotional, mental, and spiritual. If we are to live a happy and healthy life, we must keep these in balance. Most of us work at the first three but tend to ignore the spiritual. We all have a need to believe in something greater than ourselves. Being religious and being spiritual are not one and the same. Being spiritual means being of a universal mind. Understanding that we are a small but important part of the whole universe, and that each life has a purpose for being.

When I was a young woman of 20, I had the experience of being pronounced dead. My spirit left my body and could see the doctor and nurses attending me. An intense white light engulfed my spirit. There was a feeling of extreme peace, beauty, and love, and absolutely no fear. There were other loving spirits around me, but they had no form.

I felt safe, loved, and wanted. I wanted to stay in this wonderful place but was instructed, without words, to return to my body. My spirit moved out of the light and hovered over my body for a few seconds before re-entering it.

Logic tells me that this moment could have been a result of the hemorrhaging I was experiencing and only a hallucination. The reality is that I was pronounced dead. The peaceful feeling of that experience is as vivid in my mind today as it was 32 years ago. This has left me with no fear of death and a feeling that we can only enter that realm when the time is right.

It is written in Ecclesiastes 3:1–4

To everything there is a season,
and a time to every purpose
under the heaven:
A time to be born, and a time to die;
A time to plant, and a time to pluck up
that which is planted;
A time to kill, and a time to heal;
A time to break down,
and a time to build up;
A time to weep, and a time to laugh;
a time to mourn,
and a time to dance.

The longer I live, the more wisdom these words hold for me. I was not ready to let go of Brad, but it was his time to depart. I couldn't stop my weeping and mourning until I had worked it through. I couldn't forgive myself until I gained a better understanding of myself and my life. I don't question the purpose of my life as I once did. It is now enough to understand that there is purpose in all life and all of life's events.

Chapter Six

My Beloved Brad,

As the morning sun came peeking over the horizon, my thoughts were of you. To look at your raven black hair at age 18, few would guess that it was red at birth. You were an adorable baby, with that fine red fuzz covering your tiny head. The deep little dimples on the back of your sweet baby hands were replaced all too soon with strong knuckles. No one could ask for a better baby than you were. Your crying and fussing was kept to a minimum, and your smile—oh, Brad—you wouldn't believe how that smile of yours could light up a room! It didn't take long for all to see that in appearance you were going to be a miniature of your father.

As a toddler, you were fun and rambunctious and into everything. What an inquisitive mind you had! Those were difficult years for me because of your health problems. I worried about you, oh, how I worried about you! The doctors couldn't find the reason for the extremely high temperatures your little body ran. Please forgive me for placing you into those ice cold baths! I can still hear your screams from the shock as I submerged your hot little body into that cold, cold water. The doctor told me it was necessary to do this in order to bring the fever down or you could have brain damage.

Wrapping you in a towel, I would hold your warm body next to mine as we sat rocking back and forth, my tears merging with yours until you went to sleep.

You must have been around age three the first time you played what we came to call your "Sir" game. Taking a long piece of torn white sheet, wrapping it around your neck as an old-timer fighter pilot might, wearing the jacket from your suit, you went outside and rang the doorbell. When I answered the door, you pretended not to know me. I went along with the game and asked what your name was. You said, "My name is Sir and I'm looking for work." I asked if you would like to come in and have something to eat and drink. What an imagination you had. No matter what I asked you about Sir, you had an elaborate answer. It was so much fun to watch your little face as you tried to look grown-up. It was almost sad to see you outgrow the game of "Sir," you played it so well.

When you started to read before entering kindergarten, I just knew you would breeze through school, and you did at first. When you were in the second grade I discovered the school had a shortage of books and you didn't have a book to read from. I asked the teacher why you were the only one without a book and she said that you didn't seem interested in reading, so she had given the books to the children who were. To say that I was upset is putting it mildly. You had been singled out from the other children in a negative way. Talking to the school principal, I found that the school was overcrowded and I couldn't have your class changed, so I made arrangements to come to your class each day to help as a teacher's aide. You seemed to enjoy my being there. You tried so hard to make your letters and numbers like the other children did, but most of yours came out backwards. I could see the frustration you felt as you struggled with the work. What was wrong? Why couldn't you do it?

By the time you were in the third grade, I had sent you to three private reading clinics, but your skills had not improved to any great degree. Not knowing how to help you, I thought maybe a private school would be the answer. It wasn't! In fact, this move only brought you more humiliation and shame. The teachers said you were a good little boy and extremely smart, but they felt you were just lazy and you wouldn't do the work. They wouldn't let you go the bathroom when you needed to because they felt it was just a way for you to be out of the room.

I didn't have any idea you were ill that day as we said good-bye at the school. Within two hours I received a call saying I should pick you up because you had soiled your pants. What a pathetic little thing you were as you stood outside the school waiting for me. They wouldn't let you wait inside because of the smell. You had an intestinal virus and the odor was exceedingly foul. Your pants were soaked and it had run down the legs into your socks and shoes. I felt so very sorry for you. When I inquired as to how this came about, you told me the teacher wouldn't let you go to the bathroom. Your attempts to convince her of the importance did no good, so you started to leave the room anyway, and before getting to the door you lost control of your bowels. The other children laughed and called you a baby. How humiliating that was, and yet you made light of it, as you did of all the hurts in your life.

For years I've felt the guilt of placing you in that environment. I didn't make you go back to it. Instead you re-entered public school and there you were given a test which revealed your dyslexia. Your verbal skills were so advanced they exceeded the school's ability to test them. Although you were in fourth grade, your reading and math skills were only that of a second grader. Your father and I had a difficult time understanding this, and he wouldn't accept it. It wasn't long after the testing that he told me he wanted a divorce. In your young mind, you felt this was your fault because you weren't doing well in school. My attempts at reassuring you that it had nothing to do with you didn't seem to help. Your father had told me that he had outgrown me. How could you have understood this at such a young age? Our getting back together some nine months later made you very happy.

November 2nd of that year was a Sunday. You had been out playing with friends. I was deep in thought about how I could leave your father. Taking him back into our life had been a mistake. I had tried to get him to leave, but he refused. My biggest concern was how I would support the three of us. When you asked for permission to walk the three blocks to a market with the other boys, I said no at first, but then gave in to you after you told me an older boy we knew would be with you. I was so into my own thoughts, I didn't notice what time it was when you left.

Excitement was what I was feeling—excited because at long last I could see clearly how I could make it work. How I could take care of us. Oh, it wouldn't be easy, but I could do it. We would be happy, I just knew we would! Looking at the clock I thought: How long has he been gone? Your father was lying on the sofa as I asked him, "Have you seen Brad?" When he said no, I went outside and called your name over and over. I found some of the boys you had been with and they said you had returned with them, but they didn't know where you were.

As you know, they lied. You had stayed behind and crossed a busy street by yourself. Thinking you were in the neighborhood, I kept looking for more than an hour. My panic was building as I searched in vain. While I was getting the keys to the car so that I could continue, the doorbell rang. The two policemen told me you had been struck by a car as you crossed the street and you were in a coma in intensive care at the hospital. You didn't have any identification on you, so they had spent hours trying to locate someone who knew you.

An immediate wave of guilt swept over me. How could I have let you down? Why hadn't I paid attention to the time? Why had I let you go! God, forgive me, please let him live, please, God, please!

As we stepped from the elevator in the hospital, I felt a numb disbelief that this could be happening.

Surely they must be mistaken! This poor, unfortunate child couldn't be you!

There you were lying in that hospital bed, which was to be your home for the next 30 days, hooked up to all the strange-looking machinery. Your head, oh Brad, your poor little head was swollen so large that it was almost out to the end of your shoulders. One of your little eyes was closed and the other was open with a blank stare. The sight of your broken body made me feel sick to my stomach. All of a sudden I was so cold I couldn't stop shaking. After just a few minutes, someone told me that I had to leave. I didn't want to leave you; oh God, I didn't want to leave you. Finally I went out to the waiting room, but kept going back to your bedside every 30 minutes.

It was long past the last visiting hours when someone from the hospital told me I had to go home. I couldn't stay there all night. Shaking and crying uncontrollably, I told them, "My baby is in there and I'm staying; you'll have to physically remove me if you don't want me here." They let me stay and someone even brought me a warm blanket to try and stop my shivering.

For days I stayed there. People would say, "Go home and get some rest. There's nothing you can do for him." I knew there was though. I felt if I could stay near you and talk to you, it would give you the will to fight for your life.

It was sometime in those first few days that the doctors told me you had died, not once but twice, and they had brought you back to life, but they wouldn't be able to perform their magic a third time. They informed me that you were going to die. My response was one of absolute denial. They gave in to my repeated request that I be permitted to stay at your bedside. Brad, that was the most difficult thing I've ever done in my life. To sit there feeling so helpless as I watched you fight to stay alive. You were so small and defenseless.

Day after day I would hold your little hand, give it a squeeze, and beg you to respond. I kept talking to you nonstop as I watched the other patients leave or die. At first the nurses didn't want me there, but slowly they grew accustomed to my presence and even permitted me to participate in your care.

I had thought a person in a coma was very still and couldn't move. How wrong I was. You thrashed about with your legs and arms to the point of disconnecting the tubes. You needed to survive. In order for you to receive nourishment, a nurse would force a long large tube down your nose and then pour a thick liquid through it. Your little body would have a gagging reaction to this procedure, and I could barely stand the pain of watching.

All the nurses and doctors felt so sorry for you and wanted to do everything they could to help you recover. "He's such a strong little boy and has a tremendous will to live," they would say. One afternoon I told the head nurse I couldn't stand to see you go through another feeding and asked her why you couldn't be fed baby food. She gave me many good reasons, but finally gave into my desire, saying, "Okay, I'll order the food and help you feed him, but if anything goes wrong, I'll deny any knowledge of the whole thing and say you did it on your own."

Brad, we can be so thankful to this brave woman for taking the risk she did. You were not getting any better, and she was brave enough to try something different. The two of us struggled to remove your limp body from the bed to the chair, which looked like an adult highchair. We tied you into it with a sheet, and as she held your head back, I put the food into your mouth. While holding your mouth closed with one hand, with the other I rubbed your throat as if I were force-feeding a puppy. At first it didn't work, but with continued effort your little muscles started to cooperate and you swallowed. The nurse and I were delighted, so when she was working, you were fed in this manner.

Now that I had her cooperation, I asked her to help me walk you. With one of us on each side of you, we held your arms, supporting you at the elbows as we walked about the room. Your left leg seemed to want to cooperate, but the right one was dead weight. It was about two weeks later that the doctor said, "It looks as if he is starting to come out of the coma. You can attempt to feed him by mouth." The nurse and I smiled at each other as she said, "Okay, doctor, we'll give it a try."

There was another little boy your age who entered intensive care about one week after you were placed there. He had been kicked in the head by a horse. The same neurosurgeons who were caring for you were also attending him. Surgery was performed and part of his brain was cut away and a steel plate placed in his head. When I told the doctors how fortunate I felt we were that you hadn't had to go through surgery, they informed me the other boy was much better off than you. They had been able to cut away the damaged part of his brain and he would be able to live a normal life, but you wouldn't be so fortunate. I didn't believe what they were saying was true.

When you were released from the hospital, the doctors suggested that you be placed in a rehabilitation hospital. I asked them why you couldn't be an outpatient instead of living there. They said it was because caring for you at home would be too difficult for me. You had gained almost 20 pounds while in intensive care. They felt that I was not physically strong enough to hoist your body around for baths, going to the bathroom, etc. In their opinion, the emotional strain would be too great for me.

I wouldn't listen to their words of caution. I was stubbornly determined to care for you myself. They suggested a wheelchair, but I refused it, saying you were not to think of yourself as a cripple. You had double vision, total loss of hearing in one ear, and paralysis on the right side of your body and the left side of your face, but I didn't want you to consider yourself to be a cripple, and I wouldn't accept it.

In time, they came to call you "The Miracle" and me "The Miracle Worker." They would say to you, "You wouldn't be alive today if it weren't for your mother's dedication and determination. She's a remarkable woman." You would beam with pride. I didn't feel remarkable. I felt frightened and desperate.

It was so painful for me to look at your sweet little face. The left side was disfigured, pulling far to the right, as if you had had a stroke. To sit there and watch you try to feed yourself was heartbreaking. I wanted to do it for you but knew you must learn to do it yourself. You tried so hard to do things the way you had just a short time before. I would leave the room so you wouldn't see my tears.

You got so tired of going to the rehabilitation hospital each day, and sometimes I would become impatient with you over this. You never once lost your sense of humor. Once you asked, "Will I be able to dance when I gain the use of my leg?" It was with a heavy heart that I answered, "Yes, of course you will, sweetheart." You said, "That's funny, I couldn't dance before the accident."

You would laugh so hard when you saw the two streams of urine coming down from your penis. You said, "Now that's something not many guys can do." The two streams were a temporary condition caused from the catheter which had been in your body for so long.

At night, lying in the bed next to yours, I would thank God for your life and ask forgiveness of my sin in letting you go with your friends that day. Then I'd cry myself to sleep.

Brad, if it had not been for that wonderful attitude of yours, I wouldn't have survived that first year. Although you had a good tutor who came to our home four days a week, you wanted to return to school. You missed your friends. Finally it was decided you could attend school for half of the day for the last few days of the school year. I was right to worry about the effect this would have on you. When I picked you up that first day, you were crying from your one eye that would tear. Some of the children had made fun of the way you looked and made cruel jokes, which hurt you very deeply. I was surprised when you wanted to go back the next day. You were so determined to overcome your handicaps, and you did conquer a great many of them.

The movement came back to the right side of your body within the first year. Your balance took longer to improve because your loss of hearing was permanent. Your face softened with age but never gained movement, and your right eye always gave you trouble because there was no moisture in it.

As you grew older, it upset you that you couldn't play sports and that you couldn't make a pucker with your mouth. You couldn't whistle or drink from a straw. These things sound silly to other people, but I understood how much they upset you. It broke my heart that I couldn't do something to make it less painful for you.

I remember one evening when you were in junior high school. I entered your bedroom and found you lying across your bed crying. When I asked you what was wrong, you said, "I'm just so sick of people making fun of the way I look and I'm sick of being thought of as stupid. Why can't I do things like other people do?" As I held you in my arms trying to reassure you, I felt as lost and confused as you did. Over your shoulder I noticed the mirrored wardrobe doors. I said, "Brad, came sit on the floor in front of the doors." As we sat there looking at our reflection, I asked you to look at yourself and tell me what you saw. You said, "I see an ugly boy with a distorted face, who is fat." Then I told you to look at me and tell me what you saw. "My mother, my beautiful mother." I gave a little laugh and said, "That's not what I see at all. When I look at you, I see a very brave, courageous, sweet, loving, and compassionate boy with beautiful dark hair, who will grow into a very handsome man. When I look at myself, I see a woman with wrinkles, freckles, and a scar at the right eyebrow. She also looks fat to me. Brad, do you think this fat could be genetic?" With that we started laughing and sat there telling each other how wonderful we felt the other was.

Brad, I tried so hard to give you something which I didn't have much of myself and that was high self-esteem. I could feel your pain, but didn't know how to put a stop to it for you. God, how I wanted to help you!

Those two years before your death were absolutely horrible. We had always had the money for the things you either wanted or needed and all of a sudden it was gone. You were accustomed to having me home with you and now, because of the divorce, you had no one. Not even our dog. She had to be put to sleep in those first terrible months. It seemed we were living under "Murphy's Law." Everything that could go wrong did. Your father and I fought like a cat and dog. All my years of suppressed anger and frustration had reached a point of exploding. I was lashing out at everyone and everything. You were only 16, but you tried so hard to take care of me. There was nothing you could do to make me feel any better.

I was so filled with self-loathing that one time when you were away with your father, I sat in front of a mirror looking at my reflection and started slapping my own face, saying, "I hate you! I hate you! You're nothing but a loser. You're no good to anyone." Then I pulled myself together and went out drinking with some girlfriends. Of course, the alcohol drove me into a deeper depression.

I tried to conceal my true feelings when I was around you, but I'm sure you could sense my feelings of desperation. I neglected you during this time, Brad, and I'm so very sorry. I'd give anything if I could have handled the stress of those times differently, but at the time I didn't know how to cope with what was happening, and now that I know a better way, it's too late. We each acted out our pain with self-destructive behavior. Me, with alcohol and overwork, you, by not attending school and doing things which you knew would get you into trouble.

At first when you went to live with your father, I must admit that I felt a sense of relief not to have the responsibility of caring for you and worrying about you every minute. Although you were 18, in many respects your behavior and judgment was like one might expect from a 12-year-old. I couldn't depend on anything you said as being the truth. You were always very sweet and loving, never rebellious or disagreeable. This made it all the more difficult when I'd become upset with you for not behaving in a responsible manner.

I lived with a constant fear that you would, in your innocence, become involved in some kind of trouble that would cause you or someone else extreme harm. No matter how hard I tried to hold our lives together, I felt I was losing ground.

When you first said you were going to live with your father, I felt a sense of sadness. I loved you so much and wanted to hold you close to me. Loving you wasn't enough to keep you safe, and I knew it. I felt you might have a better chance of surviving in a smaller community. So it was with a sense of relief that I sent you to your father. It didn't take long to see this move had been a mistake.

Your father had never once gone to the doctors or the rehabilitation hospital with us. That was as much my fault as it was his. He didn't understand your limitations and expected more from you than you were capable of. When you finally got a job in a fast-food restaurant, you had a difficult time doing the work. The manager did everything he could think of to get you to quit. You went to work every day where you were not wanted because your father told you that you had to.

I'm sure your father didn't understand this was chipping away at what little self-esteem you had.

When your grandfather died, your father called me and told me about what was happening at your work. He said he had told you it would be best if you didn't take time from your work to attend the funeral. Brad, I know this was hard on you because you loved your grandfather very deeply. That was in October, and by February you had taken your own life. I don't mean to imply this caused your death. It was just one more hurt and disappointment added to the thousands of others you had to endure in your young life.

Brad, I honestly feel you are at last safe from any more harm. Please forgive me for being less than a perfect mother. You were so very fragile and at times I handled you in such a manner that it bruised your spirit. Oh Brad, if I had known the hardships you were to face, I wouldn't have been so tenacious in my efforts to keep you with me when you were nine. I so desperately miss our relationship. The unconditional love you gave me is a rare and wonderful thing, and I miss it. Oh God, how I miss it. How I long to hear your voice, to feel you in my arms just once more, even for a few seconds. To hear you laugh, and to see your smiling face, I would gladly give my life. Reality is that these joys will never again be mine in this lifetime.

Since your death I've had a self-imposed feeling of guilt. Between the feeling of guilt and my sorrow over the loss of you, I've spent much of these last few years feeling like an empty shell. It's as if my soul had gone away, leaving my body to react as a robot, going from place to place, doing the things which it has been programmed for, with no feeling or sense of purpose. These have been terrible times and I'm sure that you probably felt the same way in those days or months preceding your death.

Brad, you were an inspiration to everyone who knew the hardships you had overcome in your young life. Your benevolent nature brought joy to all who encountered it. I'm proud I had you for my son. You taught me many things in the short 18 years of our life together, but the greatest education I've received has been in your death. It makes me very sad to be unable to share with you the things I've learned. The saddest lesson of all has been in the knowledge that your eyes had to close permanently before mine could be opened.

My love for you is eternal,

Mom

Additional Resources

Reading

Adolescent Suicide: Assessment and Intervention
Alan L. Berman and David Jobes, American Psychological Association

After Suicide
Jhon H. Hewett, Westminster Press

Anxiety & Panic Attacks: Their Cause and Cure
Robert Handley, Fawcett

Beyond Grief
Carol Staudacher, New Harbinger Publications, Inc.

The Broken Brain
Nancy C. Andreasen, M.D., Ph.D., Harper & Row, Publishers

The Courage To Grieve
Judy Tatelbaum, Harper & Row, Publishers

Feeling Good
David D. Burns, M.D., A Signet Book

Living Through Mourning
Harriet Sarnoff Schiff, Penguin Books

My Son...My Son...
Iris Bolton, The Bolton Press

Silent Grief: Living in the Wake of Suicide
Christopher Lukas and Henry M. Seiden, M.D., Macmillan Publishing Co.

Suicide In America
Herbert Hendin, M.D., W.W. Norton & Company

Stronger Than Death: When Suicide Touches Your Life
Sue Chance, M.D., W.W. Norton & Company

Reading *(cont'd)*

Stronger Than Death: When Suicide Touches Your Life
Sue Chance, M.D., W.W. Norton & Company

Suicide The Hidden Epidemic
Margaret O. Hyde and Elizabeth Held Forsyth, M.D., CompCare Publishers

Suicide: Survivors
Adina Wrobleski, Afterwords Publishing

Suicide: Why? 85 Questions and Answers
Adina Wrobleski, Afterwords Publishing

Support Group Information

American Association of Suicidology
4201 Connecticut Ave. NW. Suite 408
Washington, DC 20008
Phone: (202) 237-2280

American Foundation for Suicides Prevention
120 Wall St.
New York, NY 10005
Phone: (212) 363-3500

Write or call for a Directory of Survivors of Suicide Support Groups.
If there isn't one near you why not start one?

For additional copies of this book send $12.95 for each copy.

Please add $2.00 per book for shipping and handling.

Make checks or money orders payable to:

Bradley Press
15111 Pipeline Ave. #245
Chino Hills, CA 91709

Write or call about volume discounts on 10 or more books.
Phone: (909) 393-2563
Fax: (909) 393-1447
e-mail: Overley@gte.net

USE THIS CONVENIENT COUPON FOR ORDERING

Please send me __________ copies of **A Message of Hope** at $12.95 each. Plus $2.00 per book for shipping and handling.
Enclosed is my check for a total of $ ____________. *Allow 4-6 weeks for delivery.*

Send Book To:

____
Name

____
Address

____
City *State* *Zip*

Mail to: **Bradely Press, 15111 Pipeline Ave. #245 Chino Hills, CA 91709**